Judgment Reversed

ALTERNATIVE CAREERS FOR LAWYERS

Jeffrey Strausser

BARRON'S

All inquiries should be addressed to:
Barron's Educational Series, Inc.
250 Wireless Boulevard
Hauppauge, New York 11788-3917

International Standard Book No. 0-8120-9849-8

Library of Congress Catalog Card No. 96-38975

Library of Congress Cataloging-in-Publication Data

Strausser, Jeffrey
    Judgment reversed : alternative careers for lawyers / Jeffrey
Strausser.
        p. cm.
    Includes bibliographical references.
    ISBN 0-8120-9849-8
    1. Lawyers—Employment—United States. 2. Career changes—
United States. I. Title
    KF298.S77 1997
    340'.023'73—dc20
                                                            96-38975
                                                                CIP

PRINTED IN THE UNITED STATES OF AMERICA
9 8 7 6 5 4 3 2 1

About the Author

The author is currently director of marketing for a Fortune 500 company. Jeff Strausser is a member of the adjunct faculty at the South Texas College of Law in Houston, Texas. He is a graduate of the University of Pittsburgh (B.S.), the University of St. Thomas (MBA Finance), and the University of Houston School of Law. Jeff has conducted and contributed to various legal and business seminars and has authored the legal textbook, *Fundamentals of Texas Oil and Gas Law,* which is in its second edition. The author is currently writing an educational science fiction series for children, entitled *Explorers of the Universe.*

Contents

To my family, Beth, Katie, and Matthew,
who make me glad for today and give me hope for tomorrow.

Introduction

I did not write this book to knock law schools or lawyers. I respect these institutions and their graduates too much to act so irresponsibly. I repeat it often throughout the book—practicing law is a noble profession. Our country needs people grounded in learning and guided by conscience in its legal system administering the law. It is this legal system that allows us the luxury of not having to take matters into our own hands if we feel we have been wronged. Administering your own brand of justice is entertaining in those late night, low budget western films, but certainly not acceptable for real life. Make no mistake about it; the vast majority of lawyers serve our society well. I encourage anyone who wants to practice law to do so. So, please put this book down if you are a law student looking forward to a financially and intellectually rewarding career practicing law. You do not need it. Similarly, if you are a practicing attorney contributing to our society, while thriving both financially and intellectually, the following pages are not for you.

This book is for law students and practicing attorneys with an unhappy vision of their individual futures. The contents of these pages are not for law students or lawyers having a bad day or two. Their situations are temporary and they will work through these rough spots soon enough. I wrote this book for those students and lawyers convinced they are on the wrong career path. The law students wonder if they are wasting their time and their money. Will it be three or four years well spent? Practicing lawyers wonder if they wasted their years of hard work. They are intelligent and hard-working people concluding, or least strongly suspecting, that practicing law is not for them. Some feel they do not have a personality suited for the adversarial nature of practicing law. Some are practicing law, but barely earning a living. Some cannot explain it other than they just have lost interest in studying or practicing law. Whatever the reason, their future seems uncertain.

Be honest with yourself. If you realize practicing law is not for you, face your reality. You are not some solitary misfit. The group of disenchanted and disenfranchised law students and practicing lawyers is steadily growing. Why is this happening? I discuss this phenomenon in greater detail in the book. Suffice it to say for now that the globalizing of our economy is changing the way attorneys must practice law. More people are competing for a living in this shrinking world. Every sector, especially the legal sector, must cut costs to remain viable. Many lawyers practice their trade under unrelenting stress. Cost competition makes earning a decent living increasingly difficult for some. Granted, your own life is exclusive to you and it is difficult personalizing macroeconomic changes. Nonetheless, large scale changes affect nearly all of us similarly. As I talked with lawyers and law students, I recognized common threads binding us together as we adapt to this changing world. We are unique and we are the same.

If the above predicament sounds pertinent to you, I suggest you continue reading. I offer a strategy addressing your situation. I will be honest with you right from the first page. This strategy requires a lot of hard work, and at times, taking a few steps back. Most likely, you will be earning less money for a period of time if you are currently practicing law. However, stepping backward positions you for a first rate career more suited to your skills and personality. The strategy utilizes your legal training and whatever your level of experience to eventually attain a proactive, intellectually and financially rewarding business career. You tailor your legal training work for the future economic and social trends that are sweeping our world. This strategy should plant a seed in your mind. Nurture it and look at the future from a different perspective. Adapt the strategy to your own particular situation.

Changing careers is never easy. I do not provide a bunch of clever lines to hook a job. I looked everywhere for them and there just are no silver bullets. Similarly, there are no resumés guaranteed to get you the perfect job; notwithstanding all the books out there saying that there are. I know this is not what you wanted to read, but it is the reality of your situation. You will learn about the dynamic careers available and which careers suit you as you work through the strategy. This means working harder than you had planned in order to change careers. However, it will have been worth the added effort because you will work in a career suiting your personality and lifestyle, a career that is challenging and pays well. If you just want a fall back, mediocre, low-paying job to tide you over until things get better, that's fine. This book is not for you. If you want something better, it is up to you to grab the reins and get working.

The key is recognizing the changes sweeping the world due to the globalization of the economy. These changes create opportunities. Address these opportunities and position yourself to take advantage of them. The world will demand problem solvers. The world will demand effective communicators. The world will demand people who are able to merge technology into mainstream life. This book showcases the sectors of the economy that will be developing rapidly and why they will be doing so. Participating in these growth areas increases your chances of succeeding both financially and intellectually. The book also examines careers that will appeal to the changing world. Those who will succeed in the new economy will be able to show employers they have the demanded skills and training.

So what does this have to do with law school? Law school provides wonderful fundamental training to build the foundation for developing these careers. Practicing law provides you with training that moves you further along the curve. You will adapt your legal training, no matter at what stage you are to take advantage of the opportunities of the future. Employing the strategy that I will set out in these pages provides you with a blueprint for a new career. Many legally trained people have successfully moved into rewarding business sector careers. Will this happen overnight? You know that it will not. Those of you that have more experience, both in the legal sector and the business sector, will make the transition faster. Those just graduating will need more time. However, make no mistake about it: the future is opportunity filled for people with your skills and training. You will be living in the future and you need to prepare for it now. It will move on, and so should you.

The common idea that success spoils people by making them vain, egotistical, and self-complacent is erroneous; on the contrary, it makes them, for the most part, humble, tolerant and kind. Failure makes people cruel and bitter.
-William Somerset Maugham
(early-twentieth-century English playwright and novelist)

Chapter One

You Are Not Alone

*The significant problems we now face cannot be solved
at the same level we were at when we created them.*
-Albert Einstein

Do Any of These Sound Like You?

*You have made it to the halfway point. You really can't give up now.
So much has been invested and people expect better from you. But
you really don't know if being a lawyer is for you. Well, maybe next
semester will be interesting. Sure, it will be a great term. You will
get into it. Everything will get better.*

Or:

*You've just finished three grueling years of law school and, not to
mention, six months of studying for the state bar exam. You are now
personally responsible for making the post office hire extra help to
handle your resumé mail-outs to law firms and corporate legal
departments. But there is no job offer. Actually, there is not a hint
of a job offer. The law school placement office tells you that things
are slow and you must be patient.*

Or:

The alarm rings and you really don't want to get up. It will be just another day of battling the trivial and absurd. A motion to argue this morning, a deposition this afternoon. A client meeting to explain why your bill is not too high. Jury instructions need writing before you can sleep. Another little league game missed. This will be another day that is just like all the other days. No time, no fun, and maybe, not a whole lot of pay.

If any of these uncomfortable scenes reminds you of someone, this book is for that someone. This book is for lawyer-wannabees and don't-wannabees-any-more. Specifically:

- Law school students wondering whether they should be in law school.
- Law school graduates thinking twice about practicing law.
- Practicing lawyers unhappy in their careers and wanting to explore something different: a career that is not so adversarial, or maybe even a career that is enjoyable.

I started law school not really sure if that was where I wanted to be. I can say now that I enjoyed some of it and hated a lot of it. Now it is all over. It seems like it took both forever and just an instant to get to this point. I thought this would be the happiest time of my life; I am finally getting out! But those ahead of me with better grades aren't getting lawyer jobs. Sure, they interview. But, we all know they are just courtesy interviews. Even if I wanted to be a lawyer, I am not sure the opportunity is there. I feel like I wasted three years. And I still have to take the bar exam. I wish I could have the time back and start over.

-A recent graduate from a top-rated state law school

Your situation is not peculiar to only you. There are hundreds of thousands of people with similar predicaments. Yes, hundreds of thousands! Their numbers swell a bit every time a law school graduates a class or a law firm lays off staff. Their current situations resulted from a major shift in the American economy. The American economy and the legal profession have never been like this before. Take heart, there is a solution. The solution is a career strategy that addresses the situation. This is not still another way to write a resumé or get a legal job. I am not providing a temporary fall back alternative to practicing law. This book offers a solid, better solution.

First, you may find it helpful to see where you are and what caused you to be here. It is true that you are not alone and your situation is not your fault, but you cannot stay here forever.

The Old Days and Old Ways Are Gone

Rapid advances in telecommunications and transportation have made all parts of the world accessible. Every society is adapting to fit into this shrinking world. The United States has hurled itself into the world community. There is no going back now. Everything is changing everywhere you look: businesses, political institutions, schools, and even families. All must adapt or perish. This means you must be ready to do the same. Prepare yourself to live in an ever-shrinking world. The privatization of Eastern Europe and Latin America is affecting each of us. Merely being well educated will not be enough. In the next decade, educated failures will be everywhere.

The painful adaptation process is underway. The process goes by a variety of jargonlike names: downsizing, reengineering, and so forth. Take your pick. I prefer *downsizing* only because this term came out first. The United States Department of Labor reports that our economy has lost nearly one million jobs in the middle management and goods-producing sectors in the past two years. Anticipate more to follow. *Job security* is becoming an oxymoron. All the while the economy is growing at a robust rate of five percent! Just think if we were in a recession! Downsizing is occurring throughout all of corporate America. You do not need Labor

Department statistics to tell you that. You only need to ask neighbors, friends, and family. It will not take you long to find some victims of downsizing. Downsizing is no longer just a fancy word for layoffs during a recession. It is how the labor force is being retooled to take its place in the new global economy.

Why is this happening now? Quite simply, until recently, the economy really has not gotten out of first gear during the last twenty years. Gains in productivity have been small. Real profits and real wages have actually declined over the past two decades. Other world economies are growing much faster and attracting capital that used to go to our industries. How many people heard of global mutual funds five years or ten years ago? We are now paying the price in order to stay competitive. For many, the price is losing their jobs and not finding new ones. For an increasing number of people, the American Dream is in reverse and picking up speed. This generation may be the first generation, that, on average, will not be financially better off than the one before it. Global competition makes the future for many quite uncertain. "Suggested Further Reading" in Section E of the Appendix sets forth additional reading addressing the changing economy. These books quantitatively reinforce what most of us have observed from our own worldly experiences.

What does this have to do with lawyers and future lawyers? It has just about everything to do with them. One out of every three hundred people in this country is a lawyer. We are not talking about every three hundred adults, but every three hundred people. This means babies, toddlers, everyone! Our transforming economy, with its downsizing companies, is diminishing the opportunities for lawyers to make a living off it. Most businesses have made it one of their corporate objectives to slash legal costs. The number of full-time high paying jobs is contracting at the same time. Providing lower paid temporary workers, especially attorneys, is the fastest growing business sector in the United States. People have less real income. Even at today's falling prices, fewer people can afford a lawyer's services. This is all too evident to the practicing lawyers who are working harder for less and less money.

Every One in Three Hundred People
in This Country Is a Lawyer

Gone is the notion of unlimited billable hours. Gone too should be the notion that a law school diploma is an automatic ticket to wealth. Clients are improving the way they run their businesses. They explore new applications and processes. Not surprisingly, they press their law firms to do likewise. Firms respond by cutting costs and offering more and faster service. Job security that comes with making partner, if you practice in a firm, or senior counsel, if you are corporate legal, just is not there any more.

Even now, and it's still early, legal firms are merging to gain economies of scale and reduce staff and overhead. Some have just closed up shop. Many lawyers lost in the process think they can open their own practice. This is the law's answer to the family farm. The American Bar Association employment data over the past few years shows a rapid increase in the number of self-employed lawyers, or solo practitioners, as the profession euphemistically refers to them. You may know some of these attorneys. You know many cannot find anywhere else to work except for themselves. In time, though, many of these hardy souls will have to find different work. Increasing legal research and malpractice insurance expenses with fewer customers to pay for them can make the difficulties of operating a successful small practice insurmountable. As with the family farmer, some solo practitioners will remain. Similarly, like the family farmer, they will be remnants of an earlier day.

The United States Department of Labor in the 1996–97 edition of its *Occupational Outlook Handbook* projects that legal jobs will grow at a rate far below the output of graduates. Further surveys by the American Bar Association indicate a decline in the real income of lawyers as a group. This is a perfectly predictable result. Competition within a group always results in a decline in the average income of its members. You do not hear about it much, but more and more graduates are working for free in law firms. More outward signs include reduced hiring by firms and partner severancing. The legal business is not drowning, but it is treading water. The strong swimmers will continue to prosper, but the rest better head for the lifeboats.

There is no security in life. There is only opportunity.
-Douglas MacArthur

But Wait—What Is Really Going On?

Technically speaking, *downsizing* is the eliminating of jobs during a set period, but not necessarily a net reduction in work force. We know the news is bad for many. We also know that others are being hired, promoted, and are prospering. Many firms hire and fire on the same day. However, Department of Labor statistics indicate the new jobs are very different from the ones being cut. The numbers show that those functions having minimal marketplace value, such as headquarters and back-office staff, get hit the hardest. The key words are *marketplace* and *value*. Downsizing is here to stay because the other studies show that cutting back positively impacts profitability over time. Most firms surveyed that have downsized since 1990 have reported increased profits after the cuts. What is more, companies downsizing on an ongoing basis realize even greater benefits.

My office needs a revolving door. We are outsourcing work like crazy. Whole floors of people are being replaced by outside companies. Then, we turn around and hire marketers and engineer types. Our CEO calls them trigger people. They are the ones that win the war for us. The war of the marketplace, that is. And, we're not the only company doing it.

-Vice president of administration
for Fortune 100 company

If you are

- a law student,
- a law school graduate, or
- a practicing attorney,

you must formulate a strategy that fits into this transforming world. It is not merely a matter of finding a port in the storm until the weather clears. It is learning to work in the rain. You must offer skills that are marketable and valuable. This statement applies whether you want to practice law or pursue a career in business.

What This Book Will Do for You

If you want in your heart of hearts to be a lawyer, then certainly, be a lawyer. Be a great lawyer. This is not a book on how to get yourself a job as a lawyer or get a better job in the practice of law. Law school placement offices and other books devote themselves to this endeavor. Use those resources if you really want to be a lawyer. I wish you the best of luck. Practicing law is a noble profession. It takes courage and character to do it right. It will continue to provide a wonderful lifestyle for some.

I started out practicing law, but I saw more opportunities for my skills in business. Practicing law seemed such a struggle. But business was fun. It was like a game. I enjoy developing strategies and seeing if they succeed. I'm not saying this is the right move for every practicing attorney, but it certainly is one to consider if you are unhappy. I'll never regret my decision. It was the best thing for me both emotionally and financially. I know quite a few lawyers that would make great executives. I've hired a few of them.
                    -Senior level executive of a Fortune 500 company

----

If you are unsure, however, you are better off where your chances are better. By pragmatic thought, this leads to a career in the much larger business sector. I do not mean any career, but a special kind of career. This book provides a strategy for prospering in the new global business arena with the skills you have acquired, or will acquire, through your legal training. A law school education is the best type of overall training a person can have. It affords you a tremendous competitive advantage. Law school graduates have gone on to become CEOs, entrepreneurs, and company presidents. The key is transforming and translating your training and experience to take advantage of the changing economy. You should be aware by now that other alternatives to practicing law may suit you better. If you are ready to go forward on that premise, it is time to see how to make your legal training work for you. Your education and training have the potential to put you ahead of many of your competitors because you have abilities and qualities that business needs as it transforms to remain competitive. Let us be clear that you cannot instantly transform yourself. There is no magic resumé or interview lines that will get you that Fortune 500 CEO job. The following strategy is a process requiring research, planning, and hard work. This strategy is also a process that has brought positive results to many people just like you.

The Strategy

Define the career you want in terms of your legal training. Show your legal training has given you valuable business sector skills. This book suggests nonlegal careers for those educated in the law. These careers are not second class to practicing law. These careers have the potential to be superior in terms of job satisfaction and financial remuneration. I do not even like to use the term *nonlegal* because it indicates that it is somehow secondary to law. It is not. Your potential is nearly unlimited and you have special skills that very few have. This strategy will prepare you for that future. However, the biggest problem may be *you*. Prepare to think creatively and work hard. Tremendous opportunities are out there.

Using This Book

This book provides information, insights, and practical methods for starting a new career. First, it looks at each of the groups: the law student, the law school graduate, and the disenfranchised practicing attorney. Next, it focuses on high-quality business careers available to the legally trained. The book finishes up by explaining how to break into the career you want. These remaining pages present the full spectrum of needed techniques to help you start down the right career path. These techniques range from writing effective introduction letters and resumés to the art of interviewing well. In combination, they will effectively showcase your skills and experience.

Success is up to you. The key is to bring your skills into sync with the transforming business sector. Be open-minded and innovative. You are painting your own portrait. Those who are transforming their knowledge into usable skills are prospering. This new world is exciting and fun for them because they are an integral part of it. Now is the time to take your place in it.

Don't be afraid to take a big step if one is indicated.
You can't cross a chasm in two small jumps.
-David Lloyd George
(early-twentieth-century British diplomat)

Chapter Two

Can I Do Anything Else Except Practice Law?

Carpe Diem (Seize the Day)
-Horace
(Roman poet)

Overcoming the *Legal Mindset*

The title of this chapter is an often asked question. In order to succeed with the strategy, the very first person you must answer this question for is *you*. You must overcome the *legal mindset*. Many people develop this frame of mind in law school. Some develop it even before they get there. It is how they deal with the stresses of law school. In their quest to overcome the tribulations of law school, students adopt the position that they must absolutely become lawyers. Otherwise, why would anyone go to law school? This single-mindedness may help you get through the arduous legal training process, but it also limits you.

Through a series of contacts, I was offered a training position with a great company in their property management group. In a couple of years, I would be making great money and living in a city where I could scuba dive year-round. But, I was embarrassed to tell my classmates of my seemingly good fortune. Even though most of them weren't getting offers from law firms, I felt like I should be out there beating my head against the wall with the rest of them.

-Property management executive in Boca Raton, Florida

I am not sure when I realized it. I think it was about halfway through law school. I really didn't want to be a lawyer. I knew it in my heart. Oh, I enjoyed studying the law. It was intellectually satisfying. But I didn't think I wanted the conflict that came with practicing law. I am a let's-figure-it-out-so-we-both-can-win type of person. I'm glad I faced it sooner rather than later. Many of my classmates never did. I think they just had too much pressure on them to become lawyers. I am doing what suits me and getting to use what I learned. I have the best of both worlds.

-Marketer with legal training for a Fortune 500 company

Do not view working in the business sector as somehow inferior to practicing law. If you do, you may find yourself working in neither. If you like to think of things in terms of the sequence of doing something, this is step one of the strategy. It must be the first step. If you cannot or will not take this step, then continue searching for a job as a lawyer or, if you are already practicing law, stay there. Practicing law is your true calling and you should follow it. You may never be happy doing anything else. If you are not one of these people, know that there are already thousands of law school graduates enjoying excellent alternative careers. They have made their choices. Practicing law was not intrinsically bad. It just was not for them. Some decided in law school that practicing law was not for them. Others decided shortly after they graduated. Many decided after practicing law for several years. No matter when they decided, their legal training proved an asset.

Step One: Assure Yourself

A ssure yourself that a successful business career can be superior to practicing law. You may not be able to take this step immediately. Taking the step requires understanding just what it is you want. Remember it has to be what *you* want. Do not embark on a career or stay in one to please someone else. How will that eventually make you feel about that person? Take responsibility for your life. The rest of the strategy follows from this first step. However, there still may be one last self-erected obstacle to remove before you can continue.

Define the career you want in terms of your legal training. Show your legal training has given you valuable business sector skills. Many law students, law school graduates, and practicing attorneys feel inadequately prepared for a business career. They think they will be unable to compete with the business school graduates. They think their legal training will not translate into the business world in any useful way. This is just the legal mindset extending further. The best journalists all did not graduate from journalism schools. The Fortune 500 executives and billionaire entrepreneurs did not all go through business schools. Maybe a business degree shows you how to connect selling yourself with selling a product or service. However, many business school graduates have not made this connection. It is too intuitive for some to analyze. You cannot learn it at math camp.

There will always be better looking resumés. This is a fact of your situation. Do not worry about it. You have the skills to get the job done. Do not take yourself out of the game before you have even played. Your legal training has taught you a lot about negotiating and deal making. Your training has taught you more about persuading people and about solving problems. You know how to get things done. Let's see one of the math camp kids get up and persuade others to adopt some untenable position. Many employers are questioning the interpersonal skills of MBAs. Business is more than crunching numbers. Employers are turning to people skillful in both communicating and analyzing business situations.

So, what does an attorney do that makes him or her valuable in business? An attorney is an *advocate* and an *advisor*. As an advocate, an attorney presents a point of view trying to convince others of its correctness. This is what an attorney does when representing a client in court. The successful attorney understands the client's, the opponent's, and the jury's position and situation. The attorney must coherently distill his or her position in an effort to persuade others. Training to do this is indispensable and translates into the business sector. As an advisor, the attorney researches and interprets the law. Then, the advisor counsels the client appropriately. The innovative advisor sets out options for the client. Business needs innovators. Innovation is the driver of business growth. Your abilities to communicate and innovate are critical to business success.

Show business people that your legal background will make them and you successful. To do this, you need to know what skills you have that they need. The new strategic positions held by *high-profile workers* require certain skills learned in law school and refined in the practice of law.

I thought if I got good grades from a top flight school that was all I needed to do to get a good job. I followed the program and worked hard. I'm a smart guy. I guess it takes more than smart. My parents and teachers never told me.

                                         -Ivy league graduate store clerk

----

Traits of the High-Value Worker

In order for any of us to prosper, we will have to be skilled in a profession that has value within the economy. This requires a considerable amount of formal knowledge, but, more importantly, the ability to quickly learn additional skills to keep pace with the marketplace's demands. The successful individual, the *high-value worker*, translates his or her knowledge into productivity.

> *It is not enough to have a good mind; the*
> *main thing is to use it well.*
> -René Descartes
> (seventeenth-century philosopher, physicist, and mathematician)

Companies need people who can apply their intelligence toward productive use. A genius without productive direction benefits no one. The vast majority of people running companies are not the smartest people, IQ-wise, in their company. Many were not on the Dean's List. Many did not go to top universities. They are leaders because they have demonstrated qualities necessary for success in the competitive business world. To succeed, you must be productive. *You must be able to continuously add value.* People who are doing so are well compensated and in control of their lives.

The High-Value Worker Translates Knowledge into Productivity

People complain our educational system is not good enough because the kids graduating from it don't know anything. I disagree. They know things, but they just aren't creative solution finders. Some call it constructive thinking. I call it problem solving. We have to teach them to be problem solvers. We are successful with some, but others just can't do it.

We need people who can communicate. You would be surprised at the number of people that become terrified when they find out that they might have to make a three-minute presentation. You can't sell if you can't communicate. Communication and creativity, that's what I need.

-Entrepreneur in the communications business

See and sell yourself as a product that an employer needs to solve problems, create opportunities, and add to the employer's bottom line. The globalizing of our economy requires this new kind of worker. Many people will not accept this statement. Take advantage of their close-mindedness. Strive to be a problem solver and an opportunity creator. This takes a good self-image and a creative mind. So, what do you need? Distilled down, the new economy needs workers with the following four traits, the traits of high-value workers.

High-Value-Worker Trait No. 1

High-Value Workers Enjoy Their Work

The successful high-value worker truly enjoys his or her work. It is not a compulsive, workaholic obsession. Rather, it is a genuine balanced interest. When you talk with these people, you realize their work is more than a source of income. Make no mistake about it, they do earn large incomes. Their work is an everyday learning experience. Work is a game providing an opportunity to take calculated risks and see how things work out. They are people-oriented people. They enjoy leading and they enjoy improving the lives of others.

It is this enjoyment of what they are doing that opens their minds to creative thought. The high-value worker views problems as opportunities, to be pounced upon. Most people see problems as nuisances. They focus on a single solution to rid themselves of the problem. Then they tensely await the next problem. Work is a never ending struggle. Rather than seeing work as a struggle, the high-value worker sees his or her work as a game worth playing well. The worker benefits. The employer benefits.

High-Value-Worker Trait No. 2

High-Value Workers Communicate Well

High-value workers communicate well. They use a variety of media to communicate to all kinds of people. They are gifted sellers; whether it is a product, an idea, or themselves. They enjoy the effort of working and communicating with others. They are gregarious and comfortable with people. They listen to others who are communicating with them.

Their ability to communicate and work with people makes them adaptable to all kinds of jobs, opportunities, and projects. That is what employers need right now: *adaptability.* How can a company be adaptable if its employees are not? Companies, even in these times of tight budgets, still spend a lot of money training their employees to communicate better. They all know that effective communicating is the key to selling their products and services.

High-Value-Worker Trait No. 3

High-Value Workers Are Self-Motivated

The high-value worker sets challenging, but attainable, goals. High-value workers know that short-term and long-term goals keep them on course by providing mileposts for their lives. The high-value worker motivates himself or herself with these internal goals. No one needs to supervise them.

In these rapidly changing times, companies need focused and motivated key workers. As a company is being buffeted by change, the rapidly changing market leaves little time for soothing its employees. Amidst the chaos, the high-value worker will perform at a high level powered by self-motivation. They know they are good at what they do and want to do it better. What is more, they feel comfortable with others counting on them. It is not egocentrism, but just confidence that they can get the job done. They might fail momentarily. Yet, they do not quit until they succeed. They expect success. It is self-fulfilling.

High-Value-Worker Trait No. 4

High-Value Workers Can Be Both Leaders and Team Players

The successful key employees work with their fellow workers as a team. They can lead when necessary, but follow when the situation calls for it. Strategic teams, composed of high-value workers, answer the needs of the demanding marketplace. The high-value workers are ready to take on their needed role. A company must be able to adjust and move quickly in the direction of the market. It cannot afford, literally, to wait until all of its players decide that this course of action suits them.

You Have What They Need

Fast-growing, competitive companies need high-value workers in jobs that are critical to the company's success. You are after these critical area jobs with dynamic companies. This is where the money and action are. Employers want to know if you possess the traits of a high-value worker. Take the initiative and show prospective employers that you possess the skills and traits they need in their high-value employees. That is, you

- enjoy the work you have chosen,
- communicate well,
- are self-directed, and
- are capable of leading, as well as being support player.

This is the next step of the strategy.

Step Two: Showcase Your Legal Training

You possess the traits of a high-value worker. Showcase your legal training. What does it take to be successful? You may say that it depends upon what it is you are doing. To some extent that is true, but the high-value-worker traits are the common thread. You must develop them, if you do not already possess them. This book puts you on the right track. However, the train will run you over if you just stand around. You must act. Knowing how to do something is not the same as doing it. Refer to the suggested further reading list in Section E of the Appendix. These books continue this discussion of the working environment of the future. Individuals possessing certain traits will prosper.

I wasted a lot of time and effort downplaying my law school education. It was as if I was ashamed of it. No wonder no one would hire me! I'm sure I came across as someone who was confused and had no confidence.

I got lucky though. I went to an interview and the manager who interviewed me had graduated from law school. She told me how much it had helped her to do her job. I got hired and I really like this job. Now, I got lucky. Don't count on luck. Your law degree is a big plus. Show it off.

-Account manager for a top business consulting firm

You Have What It Takes

We talk about the traits of the high-value worker because high-value careers are not for the timid, introverted, or lazy. However, since you have gotten into, and for some, graduated from law school, this hardly describes you. The high-value-worker traits match the skills developed by legal training. All you need to do is choose a career that you enjoy. If you are not sure this describes your situation, look at the traits again.

Good Communications Skills

This is the heart of legal training. You wrote in legal writing class. You wrote papers. You wrote essay finals. You wrote and wrote. Moot court and trial advocacy taught you to speak in front of others, friendly and not so friendly. You recited in class. You spoke to audiences so much; public speaking became natural. You can think on your feet. This trait should be fairly easy for you to show because most people know that lawyers are skillful writers and speakers.

Self-Direction and Motivation

Law school and the bar exam are not user-friendly processes. You are competing against your own classmates to stay off the wrong end of the bell shaped curve. The legal profession prides itself on being adversarial. No one can get through law school, pass the bar exam, and subsequently practice law without being internally motivated. You did it because you are self-directed. You did it one step at a time. However, you stayed focused on the distant, but definite, goal. Employers familiar with the law school routine and bar exam procedure know two things: you can work hard and you only need yourself to make you do it.

A Leader and a Team Player

Most employers have little trouble envisioning lawyers as leaders, but what about team players? Being a team player signifies being able to get along with people to achieve a group goal. You learned to be adversarial. Did you not? Sure you were—against your adversaries! However, you learned, first and foremost, to protect your client and your firm. You all were a team. Successful teams demand loyalty and openness. What other profession would kick you out of it if you were not loyal, open, and completely trustworthy with your coworkers and customers?

...And More

You should be able to show that you have the skills employers are looking for in their high-value career people. However, consider this only a base level for you. You offer even more. Enlighten those in your chosen field. Complete this step of the strategy by characterizing yourself as follows:

You Know and Can Apply the Law to the Business Situation

Obviously, you understand the law, its terminology, and application to doing business. You understand the issues presented in contracts, the basis of tort claims, and the framework of business law. You can maneuver through these areas much more deftly than those without your training and experience. You cannot disconnect business from law.

You Have Constructive Critical Thinking Skills

Critical thinking explores alternate possibilities. Successful workers in the competitive global marketplace rely on their critical thinking skills to solve problems and decide difficult issues.

You have heard it repeatedly. You have learned to *think like a lawyer.* Do not take this skill for granted. Professors pounded it into you until it was second nature. It is a skill encoded in your very core. It is a skill that applies itself to all types of problems, not just legal ones. It is an uncommon ability. You can spot issues and work to solve them. Listen to people when they are discussing something complex. How many times are they not even concerning themselves with the issues? You, on the other hand, think in a critical and constructive manner.

You Can Do More than Communicate
Well—You Are Persuasive

Let's put it bluntly. In law school you learned how to advocate anything. Now you need to sell a product or service. The method is the same. You collect and order the facts to persuade whomever to do what you want them to do. Again, many of the math camp kids have never had to do this.

My career took off after I graduated from law school. Not because I got a job practicing law, but because I finally got comfortable speaking in front of groups. I have got a tremendous advantage now over my peers. And, I've gotten the bonuses to show it. All that moot court and mock trial paid off.

　　　　　-Account manager for an international consulting firm

No Business Defines a Position in Terms of a Law Degree. You Must Do This.

Your legal skills are valuable, in part, because they are transferable. Customize your skills to the career you want. Always be thinking about how you can effectively present your skills and training to an employer. Your introduction letter, discussed in Chapter 7 will embody your presentation of your skills to a potential employer. This process of defining your legal skills and experience in terms of business is the heart of the strategy. It also takes a lot of work and thought. The process is much like preparing for a case. It is research in and out of the library. Yet, it is more than just research. It is your strategy for a successful and enjoyable life. You have seen how your skills and background give the employer a competitive advantage. The message is that creativity, combined with hard work and persistence, wins. Employers are looking for creative employees who bring new thinking and energy to the table. Companies demand both technical and sales skills in one neat package: a specialist and a generalist.

The job market will challenge you. It is neither logical, coherent, nor orderly. Do not try to control the process. Just take the chaos as a given and thrive on it. Chaos is a ready-made opportunity. It is your key to success.

This is an overview of the strategy and some of its initial key elements. Keep thinking about how you can apply the strategy to your own situation. You must personalize the strategy for it to be effective. You may be asking, "How does this apply to me?" The next two chapters will show you how it does. See if you identify with one of these situations. Remember, it is never too early and it is never too late to implement the strategy.

Life begins perpetually.
-H. G. Wells

Chapter Three

Second Year and Second Thoughts?

"Cheshire, would you please tell me, please, which
way I ought to go from here?"
"That depends a good deal on where you want to get to."
"I don't much care," said Alice.
"Then it doesn't matter which way you go," grinned the Cat.
-From *Alice in Wonderland*

What Am I Doing Here?

While intensely concentrating on getting through the law program, many law students effectively put blinders on themselves. They focus day-to-day, rather than on the future. This myopic, near-trance is what I referred to earlier as the *legal mindset*. I do not disagree this grind-it-out attitude helps them get through the drudgery and overbearing workload of law school. The problem is when some look up, they may discover they don't really want to be where they are. When this happens there are a few different ways law students can react to their observations. They can:

- ignore it, and hope it goes or away,
- panic, or
- deal with it now by trying to understand it.

Unfortunately, most students choose the first alternative and ignore their insight. They just put their heads back into the case book and press ahead. They hope the revelation fades away. Yes, the annoying feeling does go away; but it will return. It always does. What is worse, the later it comes back, the harder dealing with it will be. This is because, although they are speeding ahead, they are going down the wrong road.

Some react in sheer terror. "I am in law school! I must want to be a lawyer! Why else would I be in law school!" The circular logic drives them crazy. They feel like they have let themselves down, their parents down, their friends down, their country down. They continue on, but they have lost both their zeal for practicing law and confidence in themselves to set their own course for the future.

Some students throw up their hands and quit law school. They want more time to contemplate their future. They claim going to law school was a big mistake. OK, but now what? They really are not accomplishing anything. They are actually worse off. Before, life was confusing, but they were learning new skills. Now, it is still confusing, but they have stopped learning.

In the event you are questioning why you are in law school, how are you dealing with this feeling? Leaving law school is an option. However, as I said earlier, it usually is not the right one. It is the right option if you want to be a concert pianist, or a jockey, or some profession that requires very specialized training. Find out what you need to do to get into the field of your dreams and then do it. For most students, however, this isn't the case. The situation is more likely that you do not quite know what you want for a career, but you are quite sure that it is not practicing law. You want an interesting, exciting, and, of course, a high paying career. You are just not sure what that might be. Is this where you are now?

I suggest you look to the transforming business sector. You saw earlier how the constant change is creating opportunities for people of your skills and training. The United States Department of Labor estimates that our economy will add over seventeen million jobs by the end of the millennium. Most of this job growth will occur in certain expanding business sectors. These expanding sectors will need certain types of people. They will need people who are good communicators. They will need people who are problem solvers. They will need people who are leaders as well as team players. Capture those opportunities by utilizing the strategy I set out in the first two chapters. There are several specific options open to you that I will discuss shortly. For now, let me discuss a general course of action. As I stated in the earlier chapters, your law school training provides you with skills that are absolutely necessary for success in the business arena. Go back if you need to and reread those chapters. See for yourself how those statements fit you. Your law school education and training gives you a tremendous advantage. Use it by applying the strategy to look at law school from a different perspective.

Now do not confuse a bad day with a deep-down-won't-go-away gut feeling. Even the most dedicated practicing attorneys that love their work and enjoyed the law school experience wanted to chuck the whole thing once in awhile. Make sure you are discerning the difference. Do not let someone other than yourself tell you that you are in the wrong place. Never, never give up your dream of practicing law because some law school professor tells you that he or she doesn't think you have what it takes to be a good lawyer. I have seen too many students who could have contributed to our profession throw in the towel because of some self-important professor's worthless comment. If being a lawyer is what you want to do, then do everything you can to be one. Please, do not confuse this unfortunate situation with a feeling that comes from within you. You must experience a lingering, in-your-heart feeling that practicing law is not for you.

You are making the right choice by dealing with your current situation. I know from my own experience that this is easier to say than do. However, it is the right course of action. It is never too late to apply the strategy to your situation. However, sooner is better.

Sooner Is Better

Law school uniquely prepares you for the commercial arena. Focus your legal education prospectively on business, rather than in retrospect. The time for building a life raft is when you are still on the shore with all of your tools, not when you are treading water. Start working on the strategy from this day forward. You will see how to personalize the strategy to make it work for your particular situation.

Realistically, for many students, realizing that they are in the wrong place and they need to do something about it does not hit them like a bolt of lightning. They fight it off. Whenever the feeling returns, they give in a little more. It is a gradual process for them. I suppose it is better to realize it later than never. However, doing so does waste valuable career planning time. The strategy, let me repeat, works no matter where you are on the legal training continuum. Clearly, it works best if you employ it early on. Why? Because by knowing what you want early, that is, a high-value business career, you can customize your law school training and course work toward accomplishing that goal. Remember, this will not be some wave of a magic wand. It is a competitive world, especially for those just graduating from school with little or no work experience. However, this is all the more reason to give yourself the best start possible. Let's see how this works.

Getting into Gear

Why are you in law school? This is a critical question. Be willing to accept the answer. If practicing law truly is not for you and a career in business sounds appealing, this book is for you. Begin employing the strategy once you have decided to pursue a business sector career. The good news is that you are well along the way in employing it.

How can that be?

By the end of your first year, you will know contract law, tort law, and property law. Many students say, "I've spent all this time learning law. What does all of this first year stuff have to do with business? Have I wasted a year?" These are reasonable questions that need answering. The answer is that this body of knowledge hurled at you during your first year has everything to do with business. These courses are invaluable in your business career. Here is why.

Start with contract law. Business is nothing more than a series of transactions to purchase and sell goods and services. Contracts to purchase and sell those goods and services play an integral role in the business sector. These goods and services may be your own personal services or goods or those of the company for which you work. Contract law is so important that many companies send their high-value employees to several seminars on this subject during their careers. Familiarity with contracts and contract law puts you well ahead of those competing against you for that high-value job.

The most useful course I ever took in all my schooling was Contracts in law school. I use what I learned nearly every day either in my business or my personal life. In fact, I've actually gone back and sat in some classes at my old law school just to refresh my knowledge.
        -Real estate sales and management entrepreneur

Tort law is relevant to your future high-profile career because personal injury liability on business premises, liability associated with defective products, and liability of employers for employee actions are problems commonly encountered while transacting business. This body of law is especially useful for high-value workers transacting purchases and sales or for those running a business unit or product line.

Real property law applies to any business entity possessing facilities, such as office buildings, factories, and so forth. It is important whenever you are constructing, buying, or selling these real property assets that you understand their associated rights and liabilities. This is especially the case in businesses involving real estate and property management.

Do not forget about legal research and writing. As much of a pain as that course was, no industry course even comes close to teaching writing and research skills like that course did. Law school, beginning with the intramural mock trial competitions, turns introverts into confident and open communicators. The ability to communicate well is a quality you absolutely must possess to obtain and keep a high-value career. All of these high-value careers involve a high skill level with regard to communications. Even the more analysis-oriented careers, such as project finance, require numerous presentations to investment bankers, partners, and executive management. If speaking in front of groups terrifies you, a high-value career is not for you. Likewise, neither is practicing law.

I used to be terrified to speak in front of groups. I don't know why I decided to go to law school being like that. But, I did. In the first class, on the first day I was there, I got called upon to recite on a case. The dialogue took twenty minutes. It was painful, but I held my own and I forgot to be nervous. Ever since that day, I got better and better. I don't practice law, but I have a job where I have to make a lot of presentations for vendors and customers. For me, it's the most fun part of the job.

-Account manager for a food processing firm

From my own personal perspective, not a week passes by that I don't use what I have learned in one of these courses. Your first year was time well spent even if you are not going to practice law. Once you are past the first year, you can accelerate into the strategy. You will be full speed ahead and, more importantly, you will be on the right road! The journey continues by adapting the strategy to work for your situation and background, your personality, and your career goals.

Personalize the Strategy

If you have decided in your heart and in your mind that practicing law is not for you, entering into an unappealing business career leaves you no better off. You have just traded one unhappy situation for another. You will only be truly successful when you are enjoying your career. This is the overarching premise of this book. You must ask yourself some specific, hard questions. It is important to listen for the answers. Do not select a certain business career just because you think it pays a lot of money. That is doing it backwards. Determine the type of environment in which you feel comfortable. I will suggest high-value business careers that match your preferences.

Almost everyone, at least intuitively, knows the questions they need to ask themselves. However, just to get you started, I have listed some questions to guide you. Before you answer these seven questions, the following questions should be an overarching consideration.

1. Do I want to work for myself? Am I comfortable with the risks of running my own business? Am I an *entrepreneur?*
2. Alternatively, do I prefer working within an organization? Am I an *intrapreneur?*

Let me explain this first question a little bit. Some people, although not many, have characters and personalities suited to working for themselves. It is a personality trait. It is neither positive nor negative. It is like having brown eyes. You just have them. Our society tends to emphasize the accomplishments of the entrepreneur. As a result, many people who are not suited for this type of lifestyle force themselves into it. The steadily increasing number of start-up business failures are the result, in part, of people not knowing themselves. I am not trying to discourage you from starting your own business. Just be honest with yourself. You can be a dynamic, motivated, and productive individual working within a large organization. The business sector refers to these high-value workers as *intrapreneurs.* They are well-paid, and well thought of, men and women.

Keep this question in the back of your mind as you answer the following questions, as well as any others you feel will help you identify an appealing working environment. I suggest writing out the answers on paper or on your computer. This way you can refer to them later on. Section A of the Appendix in the back of this book provides a copy of these questions in a convenient worksheet form. Writing them out also makes you think about your answers in more concrete terms.

Please look at the questions I suggest as a starting point to assess your interests and preferred career situation.

Questions to Help the Law Student Determine a Preferred Career Situation

1. Do I enjoy working on projects or ventures that may take months to bring to resolution? Or, am I more happy working where the transaction times are much shorter, like daily or weekly?
2. Am I comfortable with spending a lot of my time working with financial models for projects or businesses? Am I comfortable using the computer?
3. Do I prefer working more with numbers than people? Or, do I enjoy making the effort to meet new people?
4. Do I prefer working with concepts rather than details? Or, am I a detail-oriented person?
5. Do I enjoy traveling? How much of the month would I tolerate being out of town? Or, out of the country?
6. In what area is my undergraduate training? Do I enjoy that field? Why or why not?
7. In what area of business do I have experience? Did I enjoy that experience? Why or why not?

You may be thinking that you do not have time to answer these questions, let alone write out the answers. You have cases to read, or if you are out of law school, you would rather spend your time searching for a job. I understand your reluctance, but it is critical to employing the strategy that you take the time to answer these questions. Please try to answer them fully and honestly. I recommend answering them, as I said earlier, in writing. Wait several days and completely reanswer them. Section A has two identical worksheets to accommodate you. If your answers match, you are ready to move on. If not, try to reconcile the differences. Don't move off of this step until you have a clear idea of the general career environment that will make you happy.

What Type of Career Environment Will Make You Happy?

Once you understand the environment in which you would enjoy working, focus your efforts. Certain careers create certain working environments. Once you ascertain the working environment you like, you can focus on careers that yield these environments. Notice I say *careers*. It is perfectly all right to have more than one area of interest. As long as you have a plan of action, which you do, you will be able to handle this. Your career paths dictate the law school electives you select to prepare you for a business career. Law school courses are intense and provide both an overview and in-depth analysis of almost every area of business.

The following is a listing of law school elective courses that apply to the strategy. All law schools offer all or some of these courses. These courses translate legal training into applicable business sector training. You will know which courses to take after you have determined the type of working environment most suitable to your background and personality.

Strategy-Applicable Elective Courses

- Business organizations law
- Agency and partnership law
- Environmental law
- International law
- Regulation of securities
- Federal income tax law
- Antitrust law
- Administrative law
- Labor law
- Employment law
- Intellectual property law
- Clinic courses emphasizing public speaking
- Clinic courses emphasizing writing
- Clinic courses emphasizing research

The end result of working through these questions is to define your desired career or careers in terms of your law school training.

Relate your law school course work and experience to the career or careers you are seeking. Remember, at this point, most of you have very little work experience. Realize that a career is a series of steps you make through your working life.

Let's take the first question:

1. Do I enjoy working on projects or ventures that may take months to bring to resolution? Or, am I more happy working where the transaction times are much shorter, like daily or weekly?

If working on projects or ventures with long time frames sounds like an appealing environment, consider a career as a business development professional or a project finance professional. I'll discuss both of these career paths in more depth in Chapter Five. For now, business development and project finance professionals work with one or several groups of people or companies to create an income producing project. These projects may range from constructing an electric power plant in the Far East, or a car factory in Tennessee, or a stadium complex in Houston. They work on large capital-intensive projects. Simply stated, the business development professional approaches the project more from the people and concept side. He or she puts the pieces of a successful project together. The project finance professional approaches the project from the financial side. This professional creates economic models of the venture to ascertain if the project is a sound investment. The business development professional and the project finance professional continually interface with one another on every project. Putting together a profitable project for the interests they represent is their mutual goal. If you are an entrepreneur, this may be the project that builds your company. If you are an intrapreneur, a profitable project earns you a handsome bonus. Your goal should be to enter in at the associate level, if you have little or no work experience. You will spend some time at this level learning from more experienced developers or project finance people. You will do well because you have the background skills to augment the experience you are gaining.

If working in a long-term, project oriented environment interests you, then you should begin building your course work to fit into this type of environment. The following courses, offered as electives in nearly all law schools, will help you gain insight and knowledge invaluable for careers in business development or project finance:

- Business organizations law (project finance and business development)
- Agency and partnership law (project finance and business development)
- Environmental law (business development)
- International law (business development)
- Regulation of securities (project finance)
- Federal income tax law (project finance)
- Tax law courses (project finance)

The first elective course, business organizations law, is a course I recommend the law student interested in any facet of business to take, and take seriously. Business organizations law deals with the structures of corporations, joint ventures, and various types of business entities. Business development and project finance professionals must understand the benefits and liabilities of each of these corporate entities in order to better structure the business transaction. Many times, a project will be successfully structured under one type of organization, but will not work for another. The skilled professional determines, early on, the optimal corporate structure that makes the project viable.

The course identified as agency and partnership law is also a course all law students moving into the business sector should take. Agency and partnership law discusses how a principal and agent relate to one another and how partners within a business partnership relate to one another and to outsiders. Special projects often utilize these types of business entities. You will be dealing with sophisticated business issues in your high-profile career. Understanding these structures allows you to take advantage of the benefits that these entities provide.

Environmental issues are becoming the largest considerations in physical property acquisitions and expansions. The business development professional, in particular, needs to be aware of these considerations. No large project will be free of some type of environmental constraints. You need to understand their effect on your business. Environmental law introduces the statutory and common laws impacting pollution control and environmental protection. The course emphasizes federal legislation because of its pervasive effect.

Foreign countries increasingly are home to large-scale projects. As our own economy becomes more global, knowing about international anything adds to your value. International law courses are important for any business development professional. You may not contemplate becoming involved in the international arena, but as the Third World develops, there is opportunity there for the business development executive who wants to pursue it. The international law course introduces you to the nature of international law and how different countries conduct business.

It is a good idea for the project finance professional to take a course dealing with investment securities. Projects, in order to be funded, will often require issuing secured notes or placing equity. Graduate business schools stress this area and you should also. The regulation of securities course addresses the federal and state regulation of the distribution of, and trading in, securities. It emphasizes how the Securities Act of 1933, the Securities Exchange Act of 1934, and the Investments Company Act of 1940 apply to modern day securities transactions.

Another invaluable law school elective course for the project finance professional is federal income tax law. This course will help you understand the effect of the federal income tax structure on your project and the individuals and business entities involved in it. It analyzes the Internal Revenue Code and underlying tax policy applicable to the project. The federal and state tax codes affect the structuring of nearly all business transactions. Tax laws affect all projects and the project's participants. If your law school offers tax courses applicable to different types of business entities, such as partnerships, or courses on state taxation, take these also. International tax is helpful to those who may want to work on overseas projects. My advice to the prospective project finance professional is that you cannot take too many tax courses.

Law school is the opposite of sex. Even
when it is good, it's lousy.
-Unknown law student

If your personality prefers quicker closure, that is, you prefer quickly accomplishing a task and moving on to the next one, a different set of careers will apply. Again, this is a personality trait; one preference is not better than the other. Don't target a career in business development or project finance if you don't possess the proper temperament. Chances are you won't be comfortable in that career environment. Instead, select one of these high-profile career positions where the transaction times are much shorter.

- account executive/marketing professional
- public relations spokesperson
- manager of a product line or business unit
- human resources professional
- property management professional
- corporate trainer
- management consultant
- education consultant
- publishing editor

The above listed are high paying, high-value careers. You can perform these careers within an organization or on your own. For now, I suggest only these careers. Later in this book, I will discuss these high-value careers in more detail. In addition, refer to the "Suggested Further Reading" list in Section E of the Appendix to learn more about these careers. Other careers may come to your mind fitting the description of a high-value career that interests you.

Let's take a look at a course strategy for each one of these types of careers that have relatively short transaction times. Remember, business organization law and agency and partnership law should be on your course schedule no matter what careers interest you. These are the core courses of the strategy.

Let's examine these short transaction time, high-value careers beginning with:

Account Executive/Marketing Professionals

Suggested elective courses:
- Federal income tax law
- Regulation of securities
- Clinic courses emphasizing public speaking

Account executives and marketing professionals sell the goods and services of their companies. These goods and services may range from natural gas, to computers, to specialized technical skills. These professionals are the day-to-day income generators for their firms. Their performance determines their company's income, as well as their own.

Your clients' tax status affects their decisions to purchase your products. An understanding of federal income tax law will be helpful as you work to conform your product to fit their needs. Many times you may be offering an instrument that is an investment security. A regulation of securities course provides useful background knowledge about what you are selling and what your clients need to do.

Account executives and marketing professionals must communicate well with their clients. They must possess a high degree of interpersonal skill, as well as a thorough knowledge of their product. They should deal with different people in all types of situations comfortably. Clinic courses emphasizing public speaking sharpen your communications skills. Employers in this area all look for candidates with strong communications skills.

If you have little or no work experience, you will probably start at the associate level in this area. You will be part of a group of other associates reporting to an experienced account executive or marketer. Your communications skills and problem-solving skills will accelerate you out of this entry level position into one of more responsibility.

Public Relations Spokesperson

Suggested elective courses:

- Labor law
- Employment law
- Clinic courses emphasizing writing
- Clinic courses emphasizing public speaking

Many of the issues confronted by public relations spokespeople are labor- or employee-related problems. Labor law and employment law courses provide important background knowledge applicable to these recurring issues. Knowing this background helps the spokesperson better communicate the company's position on the particular matter.

Public relations spokespeople represent their firms or clients to the public. This is a high-profile, sometimes high-pressure, position, where you must communicate to the public on television or through the newspapers. Clinic courses emphasizing writing and public speaking are invaluable in this career. You must appear confident in front of your audience.

A career in public relations is equally available to the intrapreneur and the entrepreneur. Public relations professionals may work for one company and solely represent the company's interests. They may also work in a public relations firm or for themselves. In this instance, they will have one or more clients whom they represent.

If you have little or no work experience, you will probably start in the public relations department at an entry or associate level. Your assignments increase in responsibility as you gain experience. Your communications skills, both oral and written, determine your advancement into higher profile assignments.

Manager of a Product Line or Business Unit

Suggested elective courses:

- Labor law
- Employment law
- Environmental law
- Administrative law
- Clinic courses emphasizing public speaking

The manager of a product line or a business unit is responsible for the daily operations of the product line or business unit. You are responsible for its profit and loss position, on the purely technical side, and for its relationship with its customers and vendors, as well as its own employees, on the human side. The business manager facilitates a variety of issues among many people. Clinic courses in public speaking help you communicate with a variety of people comfortably. Much of your time is spent with employees and workers. Labor law and employment law provide insight into the issues important to these groups.

An environmental law course is useful to a manager operating a facility, such as a manufacturing plant. Environmental regulations promulgated by federal and state agencies affect all large manufacturing and commercial facilities in some manner. In conjunction with an environmental law course, administrative law adds further insight. Administrative law deals with the organization and procedures of federal and state administrative agencies. With government increasingly involving itself in the business world, this is relevant information for the professional in charge of a major business unit or product line. There is no business or line of products or services that is not under, at least in part, both federal and state regulation. This course explains how agencies create and administer these rules and regulations.

Managers of business units or product lines normally are intrapreneurs. Occasionally, companies will hire consultants to run certain facilities or handle specific product lines providing opportunity for entrepreneurial self-employment. People with little business experience start as assistant managers and work their way up in the company, as well as into more lucrative business units and product lines.

Progress is impossible without change; and those who cannot change their minds cannot change anything.
-George Bernard Shaw

Human Resources Professional

Suggested elective courses:

- Labor law
- Employment law
- Antitrust law
- Administrative law
- Clinic courses emphasizing public speaking
- Clinic courses emphasizing writing

Medium-sized to very large companies employ human resources professionals to interface with workers and employees. This professional performs a wide spectrum of duties. These duties, in part, include training, disciplinary actions, hiring and firing, providing information to workers and employees on various company policies, and negotiating labor contracts. Employment law and labor law are of obvious benefit. Clinic courses emphasizing public speaking and writing help the professional better communicate.

Antitrust law course work is useful for this professional because our government and the general public monitor the merger activities of large corporations. The course focuses on governmental regulations pertaining to monopolies, restraint of trade, price-fixing, and price discrimination. Most large corporations provide their key employees with a short course on this topic because it is so relevant to their situation. The human resources professional usually conducts these courses in conjunction with the legal department. Finally, administrative law helps the human resources professional understand how the federal and state agencies create and administer certain employment and labor laws.

If you are a recent graduate, you will start at the associate level and take on added responsibilities as you gain experience. Human resources professionals are nearly always employees of the company. Companies will hire independent professionals to handle special assignments, such as outsourcing or organization restructuring.

Property Management Professional

Suggested elective courses:
- Employment law
- Labor law
- Environmental law

Property managers are responsible for the financial and operations management of various types of properties. These include properties like apartments, shopping centers, and office buildings. Many real estate managers manage a mixed portfolio of different types of buildings. Some professionals specialize in managing one type of property.

Property management professionals are responsible for the daily operations and maintenance of these facilities. Sometimes it is just managing the normal flow of activities, such as leasing, building maintenance, and so forth. Other times, it is handling lawsuits. These professionals may be employees of the property owners or they may work under contract. They direct a variety of people performing different functions and services. As such, courses in labor law and employment law are helpful. Large properties normally come under some type of environmental regulation. An environmental law course provides the manager with useful background information to deal with these issues.

Your career path will begin at the assistant level at a relatively small physical property. As you gain experience, you will move into the lead management role in increasingly larger physical assets.

Corporate Trainer

Suggested elective courses:

- Labor law
- Employment law
- Clinic courses emphasizing public speaking
- Clinic courses emphasizing writing

Corporate trainers, either as employees of the corporation or as consultants, educate the corporation's employees in various subjects or practices the corporation deems necessary. You design your programs to improve the employees' productivity. It may be as basic as teaching remedial reading and math skills to entry level factory workers or as specialized as instructing senior executives on making more effective presentations. Many times, you counsel employees on their career and skill development and on ways of improving their business potential.

Labor law and employment law are useful as the corporate trainer will be dealing with his or her own corporation's employees or those of various other corporations. The effective corporate trainer must effectively communicate in speech and in writing to those employees he or she is instructing. To that end, clinic courses emphasizing public speaking and writing are invaluable.

You may begin at a lower level within the department if you are in a large company. However, many smaller companies take recent graduates and assign them courses to teach. Advancement can be rapid if you communicate well and are easily able to develop a good rapport.

Management Consultant

Suggested elective courses:

- International law
- Labor law
- Employment law
- Bankruptcy law
- Clinic courses emphasizing writing
- Clinic courses emphasizing public speaking
- Federal income tax law and various other tax law courses

Management consultants are usually self-employed or work for large consulting firms. They advise the client company's executive management on various facets of the client company's business. The consultant may assist with a reorganization or play a role in launching a new product line. These professionals provide an unbiased, fresh look at the corporate business. Since much of management consultants' work involves reorganizations and redeployment of personnel, employment law and labor law courses provide useful information.

Many times, management consultants help a company come out of bankruptcy. A course in bankruptcy law sets out the rights and restrictions of the protected company. Many consultants assist the start-up of foreign ventures. International law provides a good basis for understanding how the company is to operate. It is helpful to have a tax background in your arsenal. Management consultants often assist the corporation in understanding the tax implications of a certain course of action. Courses on federal income taxation and other tax law courses are useful in this situation.

Consulting firms hire law school graduates with little or no work experience into an associate level. You work in a team with an experienced consultant at the lead. As you gain experience, you will, eventually, be a lead consultant for various projects.

If you think education is expensive,
try ignorance.
-Derek Bok

Education Consultant

Suggested elective courses:

- Clinic courses emphasizing writing
- Clinic courses emphasizing public speaking
- Clinic courses emphasizing research

Education consultants complement and, in some situations, replace conventional teachers. These professionals create teaching packages on various subjects for children and adults. These packages are usually innovative, computer-assisted learning programs that the students can learn by themselves or as a group. Education consultants are dynamic people able to communicate many different types of material. Clinic courses emphasizing public speaking, research, and writing provide this necessary background. This field needs people from all backgrounds to create a broad spectrum of education packages.

Education consultants can either work for themselves or work in consulting firms. These consulting firms provide a range of services from educational packages to the teachers themselves. Do not be misled into thinking you need a background in teaching to be successful in this field. The key is to be able to communicate well, both orally and in writing. Where your career path begins here depends upon whether you have an area of expertise needed by the particular consulting firm.

Publishing Editor

Suggested elective courses:

- Clinic courses emphasizing writing
- Clinic courses emphasizing research
- Intellectual property law

Publishing falls into two realms: books or periodicals. Book editors plan the line of books in which their publishing company will invest money to print. They negotiate with the authors submitting manuscripts to the publishing company. Periodical editors function similarly to book editors, except they are in the periodical realm. They need to understand the reading public to determine appealing topics. As with book editors, they do a lot of rewriting and may do some writing of their own. Whether you are in the magazine or book environment, strong writing and organizational skills are necessary. You need to be able to communicate with authors, your own staff, and, ultimately, to your readership. This makes course work emphasizing writing and research invaluable.

Many law schools offer a course in intellectual property law. This course addresses, among other topics, copyright issues. Understanding potential copyright pitfalls helps the publications editor avoid liability in this area.

The publishing field is very competitive. You should expect to begin at the associate level working on rather small projects. No matter the size of the project, you will use both your writing skills and your problem solving abilities. As you prove yourself, increasingly higher profile projects are your responsibility.

2. Am I comfortable spending a lot of my time working with financial models for projects or businesses?

If you are numbers oriented, a project finance professional situation may be an excellent career for you. As discussed in the previous question, this high profile individual works with a wide range of people. On the same day, you may meet with investment bankers, business development people, and engineers as you optimize the funding for a particular project. If you enjoy creating economic models on the computer, this is a very good career choice for you.

If you want to pursue a career in project finance, the following elective courses are relevant:

- Business organization law
- Agency and partnership law
- Regulation of securities
- Federal income tax law
- Various tax law courses

Refer to the earlier descriptions of the suggested elective courses for project finance professionals for guidance in helping you select relevant course work.

3. Do I enjoy making the effort to meet new people?

If you enjoy meeting people and are comfortable dealing with people of varying backgrounds, there are a number of high-profile career options open to you:

- business development professional
- account executive/marketing professional
- public relations spokesperson
- manager of a product line or business unit
- human resources professional
- property management professional
- corporate trainer
- management consultant
- education consultant
- publishing editor

As you can see, all of the high-value careers, except for the project finance professional, require you to be comfortable around different types of people in all types of situations. This also describes the disposition of an attorney. Follow the suggested courses for the careers that interest you. This is the beginning of incorporating your legal course work as background for a business career.

The problem, when solved, will be simple.
-Charles Kettering
(early-twentieth-century U.S. inventor)

4. Do I prefer working with concepts rather than details? Or, am I a detail-oriented person?

Some people are more comfortable with concepts, rather than details. The following careers are more suited to this disposition:

- business development professional
- account executive/marketing professional
- management of certain business units and product lines
- corporate trainer
- some management consultant positions
- education consultant
- publishing editor

Detail-oriented people are best suited for careers in:
- project finance
- various types of property management
- management of certain business units and product lines
- some management consultant positions

Review the suggested elective courses in the career areas that match your personal bias. Remember, these are only general guidelines. You may come across specific career positions that may be different.

    5. Do I enjoy traveling? How much of the month would I consider being out of town? Or, out of the country?

Some careers, especially those in marketing and business development, require extensive traveling. Other careers that may require extensive travel are:
- public relations spokesperson
- corporate trainer
- management consultant
- manager of certain business units or product lines

The following careers require some travel, but the traveling is not extensive:
- manager of certain business units or product lines
- human resources professional
- property management professional
- education consultant
- publishing editor

Traveling can strain marriages and families. Do not ignore this question or lightly brush it off. The suggested course electives will prepare you for a career in a preferred environment.

    6. In what area is my undergraduate training? Do I enjoy that field? Why or why not?

If you have an undergraduate background in accounting or tax, a career in project finance fits nicely with your background.

Similarly, an undergraduate education degree will be a good background for a career as an education consultant. However, if you do not enjoy the type of work connected with your undergraduate major, avoid a career that utilizes it. Try to understand why you did not like your undergraduate major. Did you give the field a proper opportunity? Remember, you are more mature now. However, if your undergraduate major no longer interests you, now is the time to forge a new career. Channel your energies toward course work that suits your personality and will prepare you for a career that will make you happy.

> *Once you say you're going to settle for second,*
> *that is what happens to you in life, I find.*
> -John F. Kennedy

7. In what area of business do I have experience? Did I enjoy that experience? Why or why not?

Again, if you have accounting experience and enjoyed it, then take advantage of your experience. Many law students work a few years in between undergraduate school and law school. Most of the jobs were not that wonderful and appear unimportant. Nevertheless, shown in conjunction with subsequent law school course work, these employment experiences can add to your value with a potential employer.

Putting It All Together

Answering the above seven questions should yield a course work schedule that covers the working environments that you will prefer. You can now focus your course work to meet the requirements of careers that interest you. You will still have plenty of credits left over to take other courses that specialize even more in your areas of interest. I have only briefly described the high-value careers here so that you can determine the general direction that you want to go. Chapter Five discusses these high-value careers and directs you to where you can find more information about them.

Success comes before work only in the dictionary.
-Anonymous

Those students who are early in their law school training, that is, just applying to law school or just starting into the first year, may want to consider the JD/MBA option. This option is only available at larger universities offering the joint program option.

If the option is available to you, I suggest you consider it. It is a lot of work, but it is worth it. The fact that this option even exists ratifies the premise of this book of the perceived connection between legal training and the business sector.

The JD/MBA Option

How to Exercise It

Many large universities having a law school and a business school offer a concurrent degree program that enables students to prepare for careers where law and business overlap. These fields are the high-value fields listed in the previous section and discussed more in Chapter Five. This program provides students with the opportunity to finish both degrees in a shorter time than if both degrees were separately pursued. A typical JD/MBA joint program requires a total of 115 semester hours. A JD, by itself, usually requires about 88 credits.

You must be admitted separately to each of the programs involved and admission to one has no official bearing upon admission to the other. Some planning is required with this option. Students must be admitted to both programs within a year, and need to plan ahead to time the LSAT and GMAT exams to meet the application deadlines.

Students interested in the JD/MBA joint program must follow the separate application procedure of both the law school and the business school graduate program. Upon acceptance to both schools, you must petition the JD/MBA coordinators for admission to the joint program. Each school has a designated coordinator for the JD/MBA program to provide academic advising for joint program students.

How It Works

At the heart of this option is the double counting of credits. A limited number of credits earned at one school's course of study are likewise earned in the other school. Usually about twelve semester hours from the law curriculum will apply toward the MBA degree, and about fifteen semester hours of graduate business course work will apply toward the JD. This is why you can complete both degrees in four years, whereas separately taken, it could take you more than five years.

The first year of the four-year program must be spent solely in one program or the other. The student makes the decision whether to do the first year in law or business. Students usually pursue the joint program in either one of two sequences:

Sequence A	Sequence B
Year 1: Law (first year sequence)	Year 1: MBA (24 hours)
Year 2: MBA (18 hours) + Law	Year 2: Law (first year sequence)
Year 3: Law + MBA (12 hours)	Year 3: Law + MBA (12 hours)
Year 4: Law + MBA (12 hours)	Year 4: Law + MBA (5 hours)

Beware: should you fail to complete the MBA degree, some of the MBA course work credits may not apply toward the JD degree. The same is true if you fail to complete the JD degree. The business school may only accept a portion of your law school credits toward your MBA.

The joint degree is a lot of work. Employers are impressed by it. The benefit I got from it was that even though neither the business school or law school at the university were very highly rated, people were so impressed I had two degrees, it didn't matter where I had gotten them. It is like the whole is greater than the sum of the individual parts.

    —Business Development Director with JD/MBA degree

Grades, Grades…

Although up to fifteen hours taken in the College of Business Administration may be counted toward your law degree, the grade earned for those courses will not be considered in computing your overall average, class rank, or eligibility for honors in the law school. The effect is as if you took the courses on a pass/fail basis. Likewise, grades for law school course work, used toward the MBA, will not be used in computing the College of Business Administration grade point averages.

Generally speaking, the following graduate business courses (your school may name them a little differently) count toward your law degree:

- Administrative accounting
- Statistical methods
- Organizational behavior
- Managerial finance
- Production management
- Macroeconomic analysis
- Microeconomic analysis
- International business
- Information systems
- Marketing

Going Forward

Whether you select the JD/MBA option or you use just your law school course work, you are preparing yourself for a specialized, high-value career or careers in business. Plan your electives and chart your course wisely. Time acts strangely in law school. During that first and second year, you will think you will never graduate. Then, before you know it, you are ordering your cap and gown.

Einstein's Three Rules of Work

1. Out of clutter find simplicity
2. From discord make harmony
3. In the middle of the difficulty lies opportunity

You're Done—Almost

Earning a law degree is a special accomplishment. I will always remember my law school graduation. You have been through a lot, but you have made the most of it. The problem is that graduating is not enough. The bar exam monster lurks out there.

You have just graduated. Maybe you can save yourself some time, money, and grief by not taking the bar exam. After all you are going into the business sector. Right?

The bar exam is a funny thing. Everybody knows about it. Even if you do not practice law, people want to know if you passed the bar. If you did not, you get portrayed as quitter or some kind of underachiever. Now, I get a lot of disagreement with this view by a lot of smart people. However, my own personal experience with people who have decided not to take the bar exam or have failed it is very clear. It makes a difference. People will give you the respect you justly deserve from graduating from law school, but you must pass the bar. Spend the extra couple of months and several hundred dollars. Finish out your law school career in proper form. You will be much better off. It will be just one less thing that you will have to hope to avoid or have an excuse for.

If you don't pass the bar exam, it's like you never went to law school. I know people who have not passed it and never mention they went to law school. It's as if they can't acknowledge three years of their life. The people I went to law school with who didn't pass, you never hear from them again. They never come to any of the class reunions. It is like they never existed.

-Law school graduate who passed the bar exam

I'm Already Out—Am I Too Late?

If you have already graduated, allow me to congratulate you. I know what it took to accomplish what you have done. "I've graduated from law school and the bar exam is history." That should be one of the happiest sentences that you ever utter. You have accomplished something only a small percentage of people in this country could ever hope to do. You should be proud of your achievement. Now, after you have properly celebrated, direct your energy to your future.

You may be asking, "Now what do I do?" The answer is simple if you are following the strategy. You go forward. The answer is similarly evident if you really want to be an attorney. You work at being an attorney, even if it means working for free for a while. You do whatever it takes to get on somewhere. This book is not for you. This is a worthwhile endeavor. I know many fine attorneys. They provide a valuable service to their clients, to the economy, and to society. They are intellectuals with common sense and people of character. It is, and will continue to be, a noble profession.

The trait these fine attorneys have in common is that they want to be attorneys. An internal desire drives them. Be brutally honest with yourself about what you want. Don't hold on to the lawyer dream if it is someone else's. It has to be your dream. What about if you are on the bubble? Maybe you want to be a lawyer, maybe you don't. If you could get a job as one, you might like to be one. This is probably a good time to talk about being a lawyer. We'll take a good look at the job. That is what becoming an attorney is for you—a job; not a career decision. Have a realistic view of why you want to practice law. The person in the mirror—the lawyer—must relate to that projected self image who was once so interested in practicing law.

If you have graduated from law school and realize that practicing law is not for you, the strategy is available to you. Direct your focus toward a high-value career path in the business sector. Take the legal training that you have and showcase it in terms of the business sector. Later chapters on introduction letters and resumé writing will help you with this.

The buck stops here!
-Harry Truman
(former Kansas City Law School student
and 33rd president of the United States)

Chapter Four

The Perils of Practice

*When you have to make a choice and
do not make it, that is in itself a choice.*
-Will James
(early-twentieth-century American author and artist)

You're In, But You Want Out

There are over three-quarters of a million lawyers, give or take, in this country. More are on the way. The law school mills continue running at full capacity. They produce graduates in numbers incomprehensible a generation ago. Practicing law affects differently those who do it. Many love it and that is great. Everyone should be able to work at what they truly love to do. Some though, quite frankly, hate it. This chapter is for the disenchanted. Various studies, including some by the American Bar Association, indicate more than one-third of the practicing attorneys fall into this category. They have become disillusioned because they work long hours and they don't get paid enough for their efforts. Every day tests their will to go for one more day. Maybe it will get better, they hope. Unfortunately, it does not.

Forget the cheese! Just get me out of this trap!
-A disenchanted mouse

If you are one of these attorneys, or think you might be one of them, you are obviously not alone. You are not a failure. There is certainly nothing wrong with you. Practicing law has changed dramatically in the last five years.

I already discussed what is going on. The legal profession is in a state of self-destructive competition. An increasing number of attorneys are competing for a shrinking base of customers. Customers are committed to slashing legal expenses. From their perspective, our profession is a source of expense for their business. Attorney and client are working at cross purposes. This forces the legal business to rearrange itself. This process creates misery that manifests itself in a number of ways.

What is it that the unhappy lawyers dislike about their profession? The polls and questionnaires show basically the same thing. Distilled down, the dissatisfaction falls into three main categories:

- they do not like the work they're doing,
- they have to work too many hours, and/or
- the pay is too low.

I make my living placing attorneys in legal firms and legal departments when they are ready to change jobs. But, I've got to say, a good percentage of them need more than a job change. They need a career change. They need to get out of law. I think they know that, but they are afraid they won't be able to get a job anywhere else.
-Personnel recruiter specializing in the legal sector

I Do Not Like What I Have Become

Every lawyer, whether as a solo practitioner or a corporate cog, must deal with how practicing law sometimes conflicts with his or her value system. You would like to take the high road all of the time. Pragmatically speaking, it is not always up to you. You have bosses and clients to whom you must answer. You do not do any-thing wrong; but it is not exactly right either. At least not exactly right from the perspective that you grew up with. It is not the big issues. You usually deal with those head on and decide them for yourself. It is the day-to-day stuff that just sort of passes by and mounts up. Like, representing a client who you think has no right to your services. This is, in one way or another, a moral question that you have implicitly decided by your action. Again, pragmatically, it was not really a decision that you sat down and made. It just happens as part of the job. Many attorneys have accepted their powerlessness to decide every issue. They are still good people. Others never really seem to be able to do it and they pay the price.

When I was in law school I was going to save the world when I got out. I love kids, and I became interested in family law as a way to help kids get out of abusive situations. I did some clinic work in law school and enjoyed it. When I got out, I went to work for a firm that does family law work. I thought it would be perfect. Wrong. Family law means divorce work. It is the only way to make any money. Now I am helping guys that cheated on their wives and squirreled away money from them. It's pretty disgusting sometimes. Some of these guys are probably the same ones that have kids that need help. I've ended up on the wrong side. But, as my associates are fond of saying, "Kids don't have any money."

-Associate in a family law practice

The law is a jealous mistress.
-Justice Oliver Wendell Holmes, Jr.
(American jurist)

The price paid is a loss of a sense of decency and professional pride. You must mechanically react to your client's requests. You, first and foremost, represent your client's interests. Then, after you have done that, and only then, may you try to right the wrongs. All too many times, the wrong just continues. Do not underestimate the sacrifice the profession will demand. Justice Holmes was talking about the time it will take from your life. I will address the voracious time monster shortly. However, his statement is equally appropriate here. For some, the clash between practicing law and their value systems disrupts their entire beings. This disruptive effect causes some attorneys to self-destruct. Do not let yourself be one of them.

It's All I Do!

Many lawyers complain the profession consumes them. Practicing law exemplifies the trading off between time and money. Time truly is money. You sell time; and your life is your time. Law firms are businesses that sell their employees' time. The law firm must find and keep clients for its product in order to stay in business. Clients want service. You must work longer and cheaper to keep yourself competitive in this shrinking world. Quick turnaround times and twenty-four hour availability are now commonplace. The long hours are unpredictable. You may be out of town for weeks on end reviewing documents, taking depositions, trying a case, or working on a corporate acquisition. International travel may add into your equation. Foreign travel dramatically cuts into family time. Spouse and children feel the distance. Even when you are home, you may be away, mentally and emotionally.

Law firms usually require their attorneys to bill more than eighteen hundred hours per year. Many expect two thousand hours. Work the arithmetic. As a rule, ten hours in the office will yield eight billable hours. So two thousand billable hours means that you must work twenty-five hundred hours each year. Assuming you can fit in a couple of weeks of vacation a year, that yields a fifty hour work week. This means you work nights and weekends. How many times has a Friday afternoon call from a client with a Monday deadline ruined a weekend? Too many will ruin a marriage.

I know you have to work long and hard nowadays to be successful. I am not afraid of hard work. But, I can't remember the last time I didn't work on a Saturday. I've even gone into the office on Saturday when I didn't have any pressing work. I just went in to catch up. I've lost control over the time in my life. My job is my life. My life is my job. The cliché of being on a treadmill really does apply to me. I'm not sure I can get off.

                -Attorney with a large metropolitan legal firm

----

Why not just charge more, so you can work less? You know the answer. The global economy has made the world too competitive to support legal fee largess. The competition to keep the firm-hopping clients staying with you discourages increasing the billing rate. The employees must work longer and produce more. This has spawned intense competition, not only among competing firms, but within the firm itself.

Billable hours. Billable hours. It's all I hear. Like it's some kind of mantra or something. I suppose it is because it's almost a religion around here. We've got an office administrator that keeps track of our hours and the partners get a report every week. It's like being in jail or something. Logging the hours is one thing. Getting paid by the client is another. I'll work eight hours for a client and they will negotiate it down to four. And then, of course, we've got rainmaking. That's what you call bringing in business for your firm. Time spent doing that doesn't count. But you better be doing it. Sometimes I think I'd be better off flipping burgers.

                -Associate in a medium-size firm

The law firm has changed the way it operates. It has gone from operating like a professional organization to operating like a service organization. It used to be that lawyers knew their adversaries on a respectful, professional basis. Many knew each other socially. As the number of lawyers keeps increasing, lawyers barely even know the people in their own firm. The personal side of practicing law has disappeared. Computerization has created the ability to instantly compare billable hours among the attorney-workers. Influence within the firm depends upon hours billed, rather than on competence and integrity. If you want to survive, keep those billable hours rising. To move up, find new business for the firm. Billable hours and rainmaking ability are prerequisites to partnership. Office politics is a byproduct. Camaraderie within the firm and among lawyers is now all but gone. There is no time for it and no reason for it. The reality of practicing law has changed forever.

> *It isn't the mountains ahead that wear you out.*
> *It's the grain of sand in your shoe.*
> -Anonymous

The Myth of the Big Bucks

A half generation ago, the attorney made a good living. The lawyer was in the forefront of civic and charity activities, respected as a professional and as an involved citizen. Now, they are just sharks and ambulance chasers. Even though their status may have changed, they still make a good living, right? Not exactly. It depends upon whom you are talking about.

Real incomes, for all but the elite class of lawyers, have dropped over the last three years. The statistical studies generated from questionnaires tell you that. Many law school graduates receive offers of only a fraction of what undergraduates with business, computer science, or engineering degrees are commanding. The law school graduates tell you that. Surveys are showing that graduates report starting salaries lower than their decade-ago counterparts received. Further, the United States Department of Labor reports in its *Occupational Outlook Handbook* that professionals in the expanding business sectors earn more money than a large percentage of lawyers. Sometimes these business professionals earn a lot more money.

We are only talking about annual salaries here. In order to get the full picture, you must divide that annual salary by the hours worked. Many attorneys refuse to take this cold bath of reality.

I know lots of attorneys that have another job—repairing computers, teaching night school, all kinds of things. They just don't make enough money practicing law. It's not that they are lazy. Far from it. They just don't have the clients to pay their bills. I am amazed that some of these solos have kept their doors open for so long.

-Attorney for a profitable firm

We talked about how this happened. More and more lawyers are entering the business. A business viewed by the competitive business world as an expense to be avoided, or at least minimized. The client base is spending less. Consequently, the law business cannot adequately support its work force. This manifests itself in a myriad of ways. The most evident to all of us is lawsuit abuse—lawyers creating work where no meaningful work exists. Another is contract lawyers—lawyers who work when there is work and sit by the phone when there is none. The number of these types is growing rapidly. So is the number of graduates working for free just to gain experience. All this leads to unstable career paths for today's lawyers. Partnership offers are being delayed and many attorneys have to change firms every few years to stay a little ahead financially. Many lawyers are being relegated to routine functions because it is the only work available in the firm. Sometimes, it is cheaper to use them than paralegal staff.

Seven Years of College to Do This?

For some attorneys, practicing law is boring, incredibly boring. The law is no longer mind-challenging concepts and theories. It is details and missed details. It is process-oriented rather than an intellectual pursuit. A lot of attorneys, after over seven years of higher education, spend their time plodding through documents, filling out forms, answering inane interrogatories, and sitting through mind-numbing depositions.

I suppose everyone needs to put in their time. But, I've got loans to pay. I worked hard in law school and graduated in the top quarter of my class. I'm glad to have a job. Don't get me wrong. But, all I do is what the other lawyers—and paralegals—don't want to do. And, since it's not hard work, they don't pay me a whole lot. I am smarter than what I am doing—if you know what I mean. I've got friends who didn't go to law school that have pretty interesting jobs. They travel. They make decisions. They make more money.

-Associate with a large law firm

At first, this stuff was pretty exciting. It was new. It was the law. Now it is not new. It is now pointless filler work. It is tedium interspersed with pressure to get it done. Many try to hide their disappointment with what they are doing. Apathy is a by-product that can lead to abuse of the client by the attorney. Stress is the other. This can lead to abuse of the attorney by the attorney himself or herself.

Stress: The Fruit of Your Labors

Time pressure, low pay, and boring work create stressful working conditions. The details, the long hours, the lack of camaraderie, and no personal life take their toll. It's even more devastating when you are only barely making a living. A sour stomach has replaced the enthusiasm of law school. The truth is, and you know it; you are killing yourself a little each day.

I wake up stressed out. My whole day, day after day, is dealing with one deadline after another. Of course, everything is adversarial. And the lawyer I am dealing with is just as stressed out as I am. I don't think I can relax. It sounds ridiculous, but I really believe I have lost the ability to relax. I can't remember that last time I felt at ease anywhere. I'm sure this is bad for my health, but I really can't worry about that now. It only gets worse if I slow down. Everything just piles up.

        -Thirty-five-year-old attorney in a medium-size firm

What to Do?

Why is any of this important? Because if the previous pages described your situation, you need to find the source of your discontent. It is one thing to be unhappy with your particular job, with your boss or with your current workload. It is another altogether to be unhappy with your life's work. One calls for a job change while the other calls for you to consider the contents of the rest of this book.

There is more to life than increasing its speed.
-Mahatma Gandhi

Be honest with yourself. If your problem is with your career, face it. Follow your instincts. Practicing law develops them.

Understand Your Feelings

I do not want to discourage anyone who wants to leave the profession. Just make sure it is the profession that is making you unhappy. Reread the beginning of this chapter. If you can characterize yourself with the traits of a person dissatisfied with practicing law, then prepare to depart from practicing law. Prepare for departure after you have convinced yourself, in your heart and in your mind, that leaving is the solution. You are responsible to people other than just yourself. However, the decision is yours alone.

When you decide to quit practicing law, it means deciding to forego, in very large part, those long, hard hours you put in as an associate. This is not an easy choice. Remember, though, you are not foregoing what you learned; but what you earned. You will be leaving familiar, albeit uncomfortable surroundings, for the unknown. Growing always causes discomfort.

There is also another perspective. Consider how your decision will affect your family, friends, and business associates. They should not influence your decision to leave. However, they may affect the manner and timing of your exit. This is a career change for them also. Communicate your reasoning with them. Making the decision on your own does not mean brushing their feelings aside.

Prepare Financially

Do not write off changing careers because you feel that you cannot afford to change. It is too late now only if you say it is. Sure, if you earn a large income, initially you will have to take a pay cut to start a new career. For many, this one obstacle may be too hard to overcome. All that I can say is that, with the help of financial planning and the commitment of your family, you can overcome this obstacle. In the long run, it is better to grapple with this than stay where you are and be miserable.

Money strongly affects the equation. This is especially true for those earning a good living practicing law. Be ready to adjust your lifestyle accordingly. You may have to budget yourself and your family for the first time. Vacations and new cars may have to wait. However, I have never met a spouse or other family member that would not gladly sacrifice any of these things, and they are just things, in order to assure real happiness for their loved one. Do not underestimate their love and loyalty. That does not mean that you can shortcut communicating with your spouse and family. Far from it; this is where you tap into their strength. Make sure they understand what life will be like for a while. In some respects it will be better, but in others, they will have to adjust. It will not be forever, but it may seem like it at first.

Once you decide you are going to exit the legal sector, give yourself at least six months to practice law. You need to do so in order to accumulate cash to hold you over as you search for a job in the business sector. Be well aware that you will most probably start at a job that pays less than you are making now. You will need to have some money accumulated even if you have moderated your lifestyle.

The decision to leave the legal profession is *yours*. Take the responsibility. Do not give it to someone else. The attorney can make a successful career change into the business sector. Many have used their legal skills to achieve satisfaction in business. The practice of law is an avenue offering multiple career options. It is not a boundary. You need to get into a career that you will enjoy, a career doing what you will be good at, and something that is valued by the business sector. By following the strategy, you will display to others, and more importantly, to yourself, that you are not making a second rate choice. What you just left was the second rate choice. It is time to get working.

For years, I wanted to quit practicing law. But each year I made good money. I also hated the work more each year. I wanted to be a college professor. I think I always wanted to be that. I got an offer, but the salary was a third of what I was making. I just couldn't do it. I need to rethink the whole money thing. That's just too big of a sacrifice for everyone to make. I need to find a better paying job that I can jump to.
                        -Partner in an international law firm

----

But, It's All I Know How to Do

You are sure that you need to change careers. Changing bosses, or firms, or the type of law you practice is not enough. This is a watershed decision. It takes courage and honesty to deal with it. Change careers to what? "How am I going to change careers after all these years?" you ask yourself. Whether you have been practicing law for fifteen days or fifteen years, you may feel that practicing law is all you can do. You may not like doing it, but it is all you can do. That just is not true. The previous chapters showed how a formal legal education is an asset to landing a career in the business sector.

Formal training combined with actual experience is an even more valuable asset. You just apply the strategy set out in this book a little differently to take advantage.

The process for employing the strategy to your situation is the same as the one the law student went through in the previous chapter. You personalize the strategy to fit your particular personality, background, and interests. I contend that you are truly successful only when you like your work and you feel that it is worthwhile work. This premise underlies the situation of the law student and it does not change for the practicing lawyer.

Use the strategy of this book. Prepare for a high value business career by adapting your legal experience to the business sector. However, you just do not want to trade one unhappy situation for another. As with the law student, it is important to ask yourself some specific, hard questions. Be honest when you answer them.

The mistake that many practicing attorneys make in this situation is they take the first job, and it is just a job, they can find. They just want out. They might get lucky and everything works out. However, that is not the best way to do it. Counting on luck never is. Determine the type of environment in which you feel comfortable in and target that career.

Listed below are some high-value business careers to start you thinking:

- business development manager
- project finance professional
- account executive/marketing professional
- public relations spokesperson
- manager of a business unit or product line
- human resources professional
- entrepreneur
- property management professional
- corporate trainer
- management consultant
- education consultant
- publishing editor

The questions you ask in determining the working environment suited to your personality and experience are important. I have listed some questions to guide you. Some are the same questions that I suggest the law student ask himself or herself. Other questions apply directly to the practicing attorney. Before you answer these questions, address the big picture:

1. Do I want to work for myself? Am I comfortable with the risks, at this time of my life, of starting and running my own business? Am I an *entrepreneur?* Do I have the financial resources to start a business?
2. Do I prefer working within an organization? Am I an *intrapreneur?*

Your answer to these questions determines the general path that you will take. If you have an entrepreneurial bent, the following listed careers, in many cases, allow for some form of self-employment:

- business development professional
- entrepreneur (owning your own business)
- corporate trainer
- management consultant
- education consultant
- certain types of property management

Please do not think that you must go out and start your own business. If this environment does not suit you or you do not feel that you can risk your finances on a start-up operation, avoid it. There are many high-profile careers available to you within an established organization. You are an intrapreneur.

We call them barrel fish. It is like shooting fish in a barrel. Every time we go to a seminar put on to help outsourced, fired, laid off, whatever you want to call them, executives, they just can't wait to invest their severance or retirement on a franchise. Most of them have no experience running a small business, dealing with the public, and dealing with entry level employees. They usually don't last a year.

-Restaurant franchise salesman

The following career paths are available to you if you are intrapreneurial:

- account executive and marketing professional
- public relations spokesperson
- manager of a product line or business unit
- some types of property management professionals
- publishing
- educational consulting
- corporate training

I have discussed these careers somewhat in the previous chapter. I discuss them in more depth in the following chapter. For now, you are just trying to get some ideas for career paths. After answering the following questions, you should realize the appropriate business career options.

What Type of Career Environment Will Make You Happy?

Please look at the questions I suggest as a starting point in assessing your interests and preferred career situation. I suggest writing out the answers on paper or on your computer. You can refer to them later on. Section B of the Appendix provides a copy of these questions in worksheet form for your convenience. Writing them out also makes you qualify your answers more concretely. I suggest you keep a copy of your answers. Then, next week answer the questions again. If your answers match, you have a guide to follow. If they differ, spend the time and reconcile your answers.

Questions to Help the Practicing Attorney Determine a Preferred Career Situation

1. Do I enjoy working on projects or ventures that may take months to bring to resolution? Or, am I more happy working where the transaction times are much shorter, like daily or weekly?

2. How are my computer skills? Am I comfortable working with spreadsheets? With presentation software? Am I willing to upgrade my computer skills?
3. Do I enjoy making the effort to meet new people? With what types of people am I comfortable in with?
4. Do I prefer working with concepts rather than details? Or, am I a detail-oriented person?
5. If I do very little traveling now, am I willing to start traveling? What about international travel?
6. If I am a very highly paid attorney, am I willing to accept a reduction in my income for a period of time? How much and for how long?
7. In what area of business do I have experience? In what area are my contacts with the business sector?

Define your desired career or careers in terms of your legal experience and the environment in which you are most happy working. Certain careers create certain working environments. Once you ascertain the working environment you like, you can focus on careers yielding these environments. You focus by specifically relating your legal experience to the career or careers you are seeking. Again, as with the law student, you can travel on more than one career path as long as you have an action plan.

Let's take a look at these seven questions.

1. Do I enjoy working on projects or ventures that may take months to bring to resolution? Or, am I more happy working where the transaction times are much shorter, like daily or weekly?

If working on projects or ventures with long time frames sounds like an appealing environment, consider a business development or a project finance career. I discussed these careers somewhat in the previous chapter and I will discuss them in more depth in Chapter Five. For now, business development and project finance professionals work with one or several groups of people or companies to create an income producing project. They work on a variety of large-scale capital-intensive projects throughout the United

States and the world. Simply stated, the business development professional approaches the project more from the people and concept side. He or she puts the pieces of a successful project together. The project finance professional approaches the project from the financial side. This professional creates economic models of the venture to ascertain if the project is a sound investment. This is a specialized career and requires a financial background.

The business development professional and the project finance professional continually interface with one another on every project. Putting together a profitable project for the interests they represent is their mutual goal. If you are an entrepreneur, this may be the project that builds your company. If you are an intrapreneur, a profitable project earns you a handsome bonus.

If your personality prefers quicker closure, that is, you prefer to accomplish a task quickly and move on to the next one, a different set of careers will apply. Again, this is a personality trait; one preference is not better than the other. Do not select a career in business development or project finance if you do not possess the proper temperament because you think you will make a lot of money. Chances are you will not be comfortable in that career environment. Instead, think about one of these high-value careers where the transaction times are much shorter.

- account executive/marketing professional
- public relations spokesperson
- manager of a product line or business unit
- human resources professional
- property management professional
- corporate trainer
- management consultant
- education consultant
- publishing editor

These are high-value business careers. These careers are attainable within an organization or on your own. Later in this book, I discuss the characteristics of a high-value career. Other careers may come to your mind fitting the description of a high-value career and you can consider them.

2. How are my computer skills? Am I comfortable working with spreadsheets? With presentation software? Am I willing to upgrade my computer skills?

High-value career positions usually require a variety of computer skills. These include word processing skills, which most attorneys have. However, they may also include spreadsheet skills and familiarity with software for making presentations. If you are afraid of computers and unwilling to learn about them, high-value careers may not be your answer.

Careers utilizing computers the most are:

- project finance professional
- management consultant
- education consultant

If you are analytical and enjoy working with computers, consider these careers. The high-profile careers requiring the least computer skills are:

- human resources professional
- public relations spokesperson

However, be aware these positions require word processing skills at a minimum. My advice is to spend the time and update your skills to include the computer.

3. Do I enjoy making the effort to meet new people? With what types of people am I comfortable?

Most attorneys have good people skills and are comfortable meeting new people and dealing with the general public. More specifically, if you prefer working with children, an education consultant is a career path for you to consider. If you are uncomfortable with meeting the general public and prefer the company of senior level executives, then consider a career in management consulting. Business development professionals and project finance professionals normally only deal with other professional people.

If you enjoy meeting people and are comfortable dealing with people of varying backgrounds, there are a number of high-value career options open to you:

- business development professional
- account executive/marketing professional
- public relations spokesperson
- manager of a product line or business unit
- human resources professional
- property management professional
- corporate trainer
- management consultant
- education consultant
- publishing editor

4. Do I prefer working with concepts rather than details? Or, am I detail-oriented person?

Some people are more comfortable with concepts, rather than details. The following careers suit their dispositions:

- business development professional
- account executive/marketing professional
- management of certain types of business units and product lines
- corporate trainer
- some management consultant positions
- education consultant
- publishing editor

These careers suit detail-oriented people:

- project finance
- various types of property management
- management of certain types of business units and product lines
- some management consultant positions

Remember, these are generalizations. You may come across a high-value position that does not fit this paradigm.

5. If I do very little traveling now, am I willing to start traveling? What about international travel?

It is difficult to generalize in this area because a lot depends upon the company employing you and your responsibilities. Generally speaking, careers, especially those in marketing and business development, require extensive traveling. Other careers that may require extensive travel are:

- public relations spokesperson
- corporate trainer
- management consultant
- manager of some business units or product lines
- project finance

The following careers require some travel, but the traveling is not extensive:

- manager of some business units or product lines
- human resources professional
- property management professional
- education consultant
- publishing editor

I will reiterate what I said about this question to the law student. Do not take this question lightly. If you do not travel a lot now and suddenly find yourself traveling a lot, it may strain your family relationships. Make sure everyone knows what you are getting into.

6. If I am a very highly paid attorney, am I willing to accept a reduction in my income for a period of time? How much and for how long?

I hope you are thinking about this already. However, it is so important, I raise it as a question to be answered. Some highly paid attorneys live their lives as though they will always have a steady, high income. The problem is that if they need to change careers, they may have to financially back up for a period of time. Some are unwilling to do this. Some are unable to. If you are one of the unwilling attorneys, I strongly recommend you examine your motives. The goal is for you to be happy with your life. Money is not doing it for you now and there is no reason to believe the future will change anything.

Financial planning and moderating your lifestyle will help ease this transition. Many attorneys unwilling to make a career change because of financial considerations have not thought through both of these processes. Make sure to involve your family. They can be a source of tremendous strength and innovation.

7. In what area of business do I have experience? In what area are my contacts with the business sector?

This question provides information to continue the application of the strategy. In Chapter Six, you will, through an introduction letter and your resumé, relate your legal experience into business skills needed for the high-profile business positions. In order to succeed in this step of the strategy, you need to show how and when you interfaced with members of the business sector and what accomplishment resulted. The more specifically you can mention projects, the types of business professionals you worked with, and your business contribution, the better chance you will have of convincing the reader that you will fit into their business environment.

Of all sad words of tongue or pen;
The saddest, these, "It might have been."
-Robert Browning
(nineteenth-century English poet)

Answering these preceding seven questions should give you a pretty good idea as to the environment and types of careers that suit you. Select the three or four careers that appeared the most often as you answered the questions. For now, these are your target business careers. You may be able to think of still more later on. Chapter Five focuses your efforts on entering these high-value fields of interest.

You have now decided to leave the practice of law and you know what business careers to target. Now, let us look at transitioning.

Easing the Exit

The best choice is not always the easiest choice. Leaving any endeavor into which you have put a lot of effort creates anxiety. Focus on your new goals and prepare your exit. The exit is never a clean one. No matter how carefully you plan, you may not think of everything or everyone. However, that should be your goal. View it as preparing for your last case. Get a handle on all the variables and issues. Overlooking them might lead to unpleasant surprises. You do not want any surprises. Deal with them now.

Starting with You

The first variable to deal with is you. No matter how much you dislike you current situation, it does give your life a certain amount of comfort and structure. You know where you will be going tomorrow. You may not like it, but you will know where you are going. That is worth something. This will change. You are leaving the profession and moving into a new career. Understand that there is going to be a time of transition, a transition period that might be uncomfortable. You feel like you are losing your status, or your autonomy, or your sense of professionalism. This lasts as long as you let it. Do not let it hamper your work to develop a new career.

You are ready to face the challenges of a new career, but what about your family? The decision to exit the legal profession must be yours. However, as I said earlier, that does not mean ignoring the feelings of your spouse and family.

Next Comes Family

Your family has a lifestyle and routine built, in large part, on your career as an attorney. Like you, they may not like it. However, they are used to it. Do not take them by surprise. Talk to them about what you need to do. Do not merely tell them you want to quit. Tell them of your plans. The more they see that you have thought about and planned your course of action, the more comfortable they will feel. Give them time to get used to the idea. Maybe they will not need it, but maybe they will. Your career was one source of their security. Be firm about your decision, but listen to their concerns. It is a lot easier if you are all in this together.

My husband hated his job. He hated being a lawyer. He wanted to run his own business. He wanted his own restaurant. But, he stayed in law for us. He didn't want to upset our lives. He wasn't doing us a favor. We wanted him to quit. He didn't like what was happening to him. When he finally did quit, it was difficult for us at first, financially, because we had to use some of the savings to start the business. But, it was worth it. He is a completely different person. He smiles. He laughs. He had not done that in a long time. I only regret he didn't leave sooner.

-Wife of a seafood restaurant owner (also business partner, menu planner, and fill-in waitress)

Make sure that they and you understand the financial situation. Many times, the family members mistakenly think they have no safety net or financial cushion. They needlessly worry because the exiting attorney failed to inform them of the stock of capital. Also, by telling them, this insures that you have taken into consideration this situation. You need a financial plan for the transition period. Everybody must understand what that plan is.

Quit the Business, Not Your Clients

Make sure your clients have an attorney they can utilize. Contact each one of them, in writing, and let them know you will no longer be practicing law. Give them a list of attorneys they can call. Be careful to let them and their future attorney develop the lawyer-client relationship. Do not do it through your letter. This could create problems if something goes wrong between the client and the new attorney. Again, do what it takes to make everyone happy and not just what the law requires. You will sleep better at night without the ghosts of the past haunting you.

Take the time and get all of the files in order for the new attorney. Your clients paid your mortgage through the years. Make sure you take care of them. Keep copies of important files. You never know when something might come up and you will need some information.

Better ask twice than lose your way once.
-Danish proverb

Breaking Up Might Be Hard to Do

If you are a partner, do not forget your duties to your partner or partners. You have both legal and moral ones. Again, communicating with those affected by your decision is the key. Discuss with them what you want to do. Understand what they need from you. Make sure you have protected their interests. Do this regardless of whether the law obligates you to do anything. You owe them that much, and probably a lot more.

Recognize, too, that your malpractice insurance is a *claims-made* policy. This protects you only against those claims made in the year in which the policy is in force; regardless of when the alleged malpractice occurred. So, you must keep a policy in force until the statute of limitations has run out for any potential claim. Talk with your insurance carrier about coverage for the nonpracticing attorney. Most insurance companies have programs that are relatively inexpensive. Get a few quotes to find out what is going on. Make sure your partner or partners, if you have any, keep you up to date on any potential problems. Forewarned is forearmed.

My partners were stunned when I told them I wanted to leave law. But, when they heard my reasons, they knew there was no convincing me otherwise. Besides, I had a good situation lined up. It was a good, clean break. We unwound everything. Everybody got treated fairly. We are still friends. And, I'm doing what I want to do with my life.
-Attorney-turned-entrepreneur

Before we leave this area, let me raise one more issue. Many attorneys feel they can have the best of both worlds and ease the transition by practicing law on a part-time basis. They make a little money while they are working on their new career. This sounds like a good idea. It really is not. Practicing law and starting a new career are both activities that require your focused attention. If you try to do both, you will do both poorly. I know I will get some disagreement on this. I personally know some attorneys that have gone this route. The stress was worse than when they just practiced law full-time. Employing the strategy is easier when you focus on just one goal. You might be different and many people disagree with me on this point. However, I strongly suggest you avoid this course of action.

One Last Look

That should about do it. Again, make sure you have adequately addressed the following people:

- family
- partners and associates
- clients

Do not let an exciting future be ruined by a mistake from your past. Many lawyers specialize in assisting attorneys desiring to exit the legal profession. I suggest you look into using their services. You have worked hard to get a new career. You worked too hard at your previous one to let it ruin your plans. If you are unsure about some facet of your exit, get some good help. Section E of the Appendix sets out suggested further readings that discuss making the transition from practicing attorney to another career path.

You have put in the time and effort to make sure your exit did not disrupt the lives of people about whom you care. The way is clear now to pursue your new career. It is up to you to make it work. Work hard and use what you have learned to make your new life rewarding in every way. Your horizon is wherever you want it to be!

Imagination is more powerful than knowledge.
-Albert Einstein

Chapter Five

Research and Redevelopment

It is your work in life that is
the ultimate seduction.
-Pablo Picasso

Only Uncertainty Is Certain

The restructuring of the world political and economic order is creating new opportunities for those willing to take advantage of them. Likewise, the changing world order will create problems for many who cannot come to grips with the rapid and seemingly chaotic change. Boom and bust economic cycles will continue through the millennium. The economy will experience a sequence of high growth times interspersed with flat or negative growth periods. This will, in turn, create a great deal of uncertainty for planning individual lifestyles and careers. The key to dealing with the uncertainty is to accept it as a given. Once you have accepted it, then take advantage of it.

Take advantage of the chaos by getting yourself into a career in a field with a company that thrives in the chaos. I refer to these growth fields as *high-value* fields. Similarly, I refer to the companies leading the pack as *leading edge* companies. It is this high-value field/high-value career/leading edge company combination that helps you take advantage of the changing world while the rest of the people are wringing their hands. Let us see how all this works.

If you are just beginning to think about a career choice outside of the traditional practice of law, you may be uncertain as to just where to start. I understand your uncertainty. However, judging from the experience of those who have chosen this career path before you, only your imagination and your goals will limit your choices.

At least twenty-five percent of law school graduates do not practice law. They work at careers like: president of the United States, CEOs of major corporations, entrepreneurs, investment executives, marketing executives, and general managers, to name a few. These are certainly not second rate jobs! Now, again, most of you will not be able to step into the upper echelon of these careers. However, you will be able to get a good start down the career path. This chapter sets out some high-value careers available to the legally trained. These careers will increase in value as the economy accelerates its transforming process. You advance relative to your peers in the sector; however, because you are in a high-value career, you are still accelerating past the rest of the work force that are in slow-growth fields.

Identifying High-Value Fields

If you are a law student, you have already started employing the strategy by selecting law school elective courses that fit with high-value careers that interested you. As a practicing attorney, you will see how to relate your training *and* your experience to these high-value fields. I will talk more about these high-value careers later in this chapter. However, let us back up and examine some high-value fields. Department of Labor studies, as well as some private sector studies, indicate the following areas of the economy will grow rapidly over the next five to fifteen years. These sectors will be booming through the millennium. For additional information on these fields beyond what is presented on the following pages, refer to "Suggested Further Reading" in Section E of the Appendix.

- Information technology
- Telecommunications
- Packaging science
- Energy/environmental
- Real estate
- Biotechnology
- Import/export
- Private sector education

Read through these synopses on the high-value fields with an eye toward your particular skills and interests.

Information Technology

Even though we live in the Information Age, the general population is only beginning to use computers. Not everyone is surfing the Internet. Information technology is still a crawling infant. Most individuals do not yet own a home computer and many small businesses are just now beginning to computerize. As these individuals and small businesses embrace computers, this field will explode. Obviously, this sector needs technical and analytical support. However, this is only part of the demand equation. Marketing and servicing customers will be critical to their adopting the technology. Skills in analyzing and communicating, combined with knowing the business and the technical aspect of the systems, add value. Success results from convincing the general populace that this new technology will improve their lives, and at a cost they can afford. Or better yet, they cannot afford to be without it.

Information technology connects closely with the high-profile field I will discuss next, telecommunications. Information will replace the old labor, land, and capital concept. Those entities that control and know how to distribute information will thrive. Companies will demand workers that can help them do this. Use the information in the next chapter to find out more about this sector. Information is an integral part of every business. Be open to where this field can take you.

Telecommunications

As I stated above, information and telecommunications depend on and support one another. Success in the global economy depends upon communicating information quickly and cost-effectively. Large businesses will do what it takes in this area if they want to compete. As with the information technology field, small businesses and individuals have still not embraced the newest telecommunication technologies. As they do, this industry will grow geometrically. As the entire world joins in, the growth will be staggering. Again, technical support and scientific innovation are only part of the equation. This field will need people that can communicate with customers. They will have to analyze the customers' needs to be able to bring this new technology into the home and businesses of not only people of this country, but the entire world.

Telecommunications is a field that feeds itself. People realize the importance of telecommunications in their lives and how it affects their livelihood. However, many are not quite sure how to integrate this developing technology into their lives. The field is actually innovating faster than people are absorbing the products. Companies in this field realize the key to their success is making people and businesses comfortable with the new technology. They need educated people with interpersonal skills to turn the innovation into income. Advances in telecommunications affect every business. Read through the information sources on this field set out in the next chapter to see if this field interests you.

Don't compromise yourself. You are all you've got.
-Janis Joplin
(Queen of 1970s Rock 'n' Roll)

Packaging Science

This is an area most people do not think about. You do not notice it because it is so pervasive. It is high tech. It is low tech. No matter how you look at it, it is a rapidly growing, value-added business sector. As the population of this country and the world grows, preserving the environment must remain a high priority. We are increasingly burdening our economy with the cost of disposing, sorting, and recycling. We need innovative processes in this area to service both economic growth and environmental protection requirements.

In order to strike this balance, new technology capable of making packaging with less pollution, and yet cost-effectively, will be demanded. The public and private sector will invest in large-scale plants and distribution networks. Individuals comfortable in the investment and finance area, as well as marketing and public relations fields, will prosper as this sector emerges. Be open-minded about this field. Many people do not know anything about this field and dismiss it as a dying business that does not need high-skill type people. Nothing could be further from the truth. All products require packaging of some type. This allows you to involve yourself in all different types of fields and businesses. Peruse the suggested sources attributable to this field in the next chapter to understand how broad of a spectrum this field covers.

Energy/Environmental

Growing world economies need fueling. Resources such as oil, electricity, nuclear power, and natural gas are now interchangeable energy sources. With an eye toward controlling pollution, we will spend enormous sums of money to keep the world economies running. The energy business will globalize even more in the coming years. This expansion will require large-scale capital investment and asset management. Countries, through the private sector, will build power plants all over the world along with new pipelines and electricity grid systems. Innovation and technology will transform this sector unrecognizably over the coming decade. All types of high-profile positions in finance, real estate, and marketing will emerge.

If you want to go where the money flows to, the energy field needs and absorbs tremendous amounts of capital. Countries and companies are demanding skilled people, especially those who can put the pieces of an energy project together. As with many of these high-profile fields, energy use cuts across all businesses and industries. This field allows you to take part in different sectors of business.

The energy field and the environmental field affect one another. Capital will move from one to the other as the world tries to balance growth and the environment. The skilled communicator with interpersonal skills will provide the link between these fast growing fields. The opportunities grow with every new technology. Review the materials on this field in the next chapter to see if this field interests you.

Biotechnology

This field will drive the burgeoning health care industry. It will bear the fastest growing companies in the economy in the next decade. Most people look at this sector as just a bunch of companies with research labs. It is true that this sector is research oriented. However, marketing, public relations, investment, and finance will play major roles as this sector ascends in prominence. You will interface with the public, business, and financial groups promoting the wonder products of these labs. You avail the public to these research breakthroughs. This availability creates revenues to fund further research.

The biotechnology stocks are now a force of their own in the stock market. Less than a decade ago, no one had even heard of them. These biotech firms have a lot of investment capital waiting in the wings for a discovery. The biotechnology industry, as with the other high technology industries, must learn to interface better with the general public if they are going to gain acceptance for their products. They need educated people to inform the public of the availability of their products. If you enjoy being on the leading edge of things, this field may be for you.

You have to know what you want to get.
-Gertrude Stein

Real Estate

Changing demographics and planned communities with commerce centers will activate the real estate sector. Skilled professionals will manage the newly created properties and attract capital for new projects. The next decade will be one of high mobility as Americans move away from taxes and crime, but also move toward jobs. High-value business sectors will be building state-of-the art complexes and the no-growth industries will be divesting themselves of costly, outdated properties. This shifting will create value on both sides of the transaction for property management and investment people.

The skilled individual that can marry the real estate market with the investment community adds value to his or her company and his or her own resumé. This field suits both intrapreneurs and entrepreneurs. Look to this field to create a disproportionately large percentage of the new wealthy.

Import/Export

Go into any store in this country and flip over some of the merchandise. Chances are very good that we did not make it here. Import/export companies handle these goods. Low cost bulk transportation has opened the world to commerce. This sector, like the others mentioned thus far, is in its infancy stages. Companies ship components for more complex items, like cars and airplanes, all over the world for assembly. The assemblers ship the finished products to destination markets. This sector is marketing, contracts, public relations, and investments all rolled into one. It is a place for both entrepreneurs and giant corporations to carve out a market.

I have seen people put together multimillion dollar deals in a matter of minutes just using a phone and a fax machine. They had the contacts and the ability to persuade people. On the flip side, however, many companies have unsuccessfully spent years and millions of dollars trying to attract foreign business. This field is unpredictable yet lucrative. This creates opportunity. If this type of environment appeals to you, take a look at the suggested materials on this field listed in the next chapter.

Private Sector-Created Educational Packages

Education is being privatized and specialized. Unwieldy bureaucracies will no longer totally control educating students at the primary and secondary school level. Both parents and teachers will seek assistance from the innovative private sector. Packaged teaching programs, many of them designed for self-directed study on a computer, will be created to satisfy the demand for accelerated learning techniques. What is more, their very existence will create their own demand. Such self-directed study through private sector created programs will augment, and many times replace, the traditional teacher. As they prove their effectiveness, more parents and schools will purchase these innovative learning tools. This industry will combine computer high technology, subject matter knowledge, and innovative teaching skills. Many of the best computer software people, communications experts, and teachers will congregate to this lucrative industry.

> *Make money and the whole world will*
> *conspire to call you a gentleman.*
> -Mark Twain

These are the growth areas for the new millennium. Other areas will emerge that we do not even know about now. You can have a high-profile career apart from these fields and still do fabulously well. It is just that you do not get the benefit of being in a high-value career in a high-value field.

Cultivating Your Field of Dreams

We talked about careers earlier when you were setting out your course strategy. We briefly went over the careers in the preceding chapter because it was important to introduce these careers so that you could select your courses to target careers of interest. You can design a course of study to fit a career. However, your field of interest is just that: a field that interests you. The preceding fields will undergo dynamic expansion over the next decade or two. Which ones interest you? As with careers, it is perfectly fine to find more than one field interesting.

You may not know much about these fields. You may not have even heard of some of the high technology fields. You may not have thought of the simpler fields, such as packaging, as a growth field. Review the discussions of the fields and select one or more that interest you. I suggest using the information sources in the next chapter to do some follow up research. Now is the time to discover your likes and dislikes, not after you have been working in the field for a few years. Now, let us go back and take a closer look at the *high-value careers.*

Most graduates set their sights too low. All they want is a job. They'll worry about their career later. Well, later has a way of getting here pretty quickly and they still do not have a career. All they have is a job they do not like or one that does not pay enough. And for most of them, it is a job that is both of those things. Then, they come to me and expect me to make it better. They should have started working on their careers much earlier. It is such a shame to see bright people with degrees from good schools in this situation.

-Counselor for an employment agency

Identifying High-Value Careers

To pull the slingshot back still more before releasing, high-profile careers need to be identified. A *high-value career* is a job function that adds to the employer's bottom line; either by creating new products or processes or by solving problems. It is a front line job rather than a back office administrative one. Recall that back office administrative jobs are bearing the brunt of downsizing going on in this country. A high-value career is the type of career you want. These careers will intellectually challenge you and reward you financially. The legally trained adapt easily to the following high-profile careers:

- business development professional
- project finance professional
- account executive/marketing professional
- public relations
- manager of a business unit or product line
- human resources
- entrepreneur
- property manager
- corporate trainer
- management consultant
- education consultant
- publishing editor

I talked about these careers just enough in the preceding chapter to help you with your course selection. Look at them in a little more detail. Examine these high-value careers and make sure you know which ones suit your interests and skills. I am talking about more than jobs. These are career paths. The more business experience you have, the farther down the path you can enter. No matter where you may start on the path, the most important thing is to get on it in the first place.

Business Development Professionals

Business development professionals put together projects in which their company can invest. These projects are investments that yield an attractive return on the invested capital. These returns show up in future earnings of the company. Business development is the engine of commerce because new projects and products replenish a firm's earnings. Earnings determine, in large part, the value of the company. In this manner, business development professionals perform extremely important functions. Coincidentally, the company pays them handsomely when they perform well.

In a nutshell, as a business development executive, you do deals. You see moneymaking opportunities for your company or client where others do not. Alternatively, you follow through on a recognized opportunity before your competitors do. This career requires high energy and persistence combined with communication and people skills. This is not your career if you want to sit behind a desk from eight to five shuffling papers. You interface with company personnel, as well as potential business partners, customers, and members of the financial community to get the deal done. You are the catalyst that makes all the elements positively react with one another.

> *Most of my ideas belonged to other people*
> *who didn't bother to develop them.*
> -Thomas Edison

As a business developer, you create the projects that may not generate income for a few years. However, these projects are what makes the company an ongoing entity. The investment community shows particular interest in new projects and rewards those companies that are always bringing in new ones. The projects you work on could be anything and anywhere. You might be building a power plant outside of Paris or working on a liquefied natural gas terminal in Saudi Arabia. This means you work with many different types of people. Your job is never boring. However, it is often stressful. This is often the case when a project that you have been trying to put together for months looks like it is not going to happen. You feel like you wasted that time. However, you didn't. Even though this project did not come together, you gained some experience in a certain area. In addition, and probably more importantly, you made some contacts. These contacts not only give you a chance to put together a future project, but also to further your career.

I just spent six weeks in Hong Kong working on a joint venture deal to manufacture computer components. At first, I wasn't too wild about going overseas. But, a couple of days after I got there, I began to really warm up to the whole thing. And, by the end of my stay, I didn't want to leave. It was one of those lifetime experiences; the culture, the food, the sights. Not to mention the big bonus I got for getting the thing closed. This kind of work isn't for everybody, but for me, it beats working as a temporary lawyer somewhere.

-Business development professional for
an international computer firm

Business development careers usually require a lot of traveling. As I noted earlier, the next project could be anywhere in the world. The business development professional is a true intrapreneur. You rely on your own instincts, and headquarters management relies on you, to bring in the projects. The personal rewards for bringing in a large project are lucrative. Bonuses in multiples of your salary are not out of the realm of possibility. The entrepreneur approaches this job somewhat differently. He or she brings projects to the attention of the appropriate companies. The entrepreneur's reward is usually a percentage of the project's revenues. This percentage could amount to millions of dollars over the lifetime of the project

----

I spent several years as a consultant helping various large corporations put together huge energy projects. I made a good living at it and the work was interesting. However, I realized that I could do more than just help put the projects together. I knew how to bring the ideas, the parties, and the capital together. It took me a couple of years and a few tries, but I originated a projected and sold it. I kept five percent for myself. I'll be getting money from this project for the next fifteen years.

-Attorney turned consultant turned
entrepreneur business developer

Project Finance Professional

The expanding global economy will intensify the demand for capital. It will be up to the project finance professional to attract capital and utilize it optimally so that your company or project can go forward. It will be lack of capital that will throttle the rapid global growth. Companies unable to attract capital will see their growth throttled. This capital competition will make those of you who can amass it very valuable. Opportunities abound throughout the entire range of capital investing, from the venture capital company to the local savings and loan association.

Working in New York City takes some getting used to when you were born, raised, and went to law school in west Texas. The good part is that I do not spend a lot of time here. I am on a team that puts investment capital together with what we think are solid, high-return business ventures. It's contracts and rate of return. That's what the job boils down to. Making everyone feel comfortable that they are going to get what they bargained for. At times, the job is almost overwhelming; but it pays well. Very well.

-Finance team member with a
major investment banking firm

This career is more than mere number crunching; armies of overworked analysts do that. This is not to say that you should not be comfortable with computers and financial calculations, but it is not the main part of your job. You are a facilitator, communicator, and a salesperson. You will succeed in this field if you can interact easily with people. Investors need to be at ease and confident. You work closely with the business development people, providing the capital to their assets and expertise. Once the business developer identifies the project, you come in and set up the economic parameters that make it economically attractive.

As with the business development professional, you travel a lot while you are putting the project together. The exploding foreign sector demands international travel. This can mean a lot of time away from home as you travel the world meeting with key parties in the project. Your communications skills serve you well as you interface with professionals from all different business sectors. You meet with members of the financial community to present the project to them if your company needs them to partially fund the project. You must also present the project to senior management. They must be comfortable allowing their company to take an equity position in the project. As with the business development professional, the project finance professional can earn huge bonuses depending upon the size of the project.

Account Executives/Marketing Professionals

Rising domestic and international competition increases the importance of marketing research and strategy and of an effective sales program for your products and services. Marketing and selling are art forms. You paint a picture or tell a story about how your product or service benefits a potential buyer. Depending upon the size of the company, the same person may be both an account executive and a marketing professional. The smaller the company, the more likely it is one person takes on both the sales and marketing responsibilities. Larger companies usually separate the two functions. The marketing executive's work breaks down into three separate, but interrelated, activities:

- identify customers/markets
- devise a market strategy to focus on attaining market share or high sales margins
- implement the strategy and service the customer/market

The work of the marketers is iterative. They identify customers for new products from their existing customer base, as well as from any new markets. Identifying customers/markets requires researching the markets. Legal training, with its emphasis on research, obviously is a benefit here. Marketers also monitor their existing product accounts themselves, or through the account executives, to insure they are focusing on what the customers want from their product or service.

The first step is defining and identifying the customers/markets. Once the team has completed this task, marketing professionals formulate how to focus the markets' attention on the company's goods and services. To effectively do this, they have to know what it is customers want and how to show the product in that light. The marketing strategy must take into account the combined capacities of sales, advertising, and public relations departments. A sound marketing strategy is important not only for new goods and services but also for established lines. Sales generate the cash that keeps the company going and provide the company with the capital to grow.

Once the marketing program is underway, the account executives in the sales department take over. They develop and implement a sales program. Sales managers define territories, set sales goals, and oversee training programs for sales staff. They contact and cultivate the targeted customer base. This interfacing of sales personnel with customers generates the company's income. All of the manufacturing know-how, advertising expenditures, and marketing strategies mean nothing if the goods or services do not get sold. An essential part of the work of executives and managers in sales involves maintaining good relations with clients and customers. These clients and customers may include other corporations, foreign governments, and suppliers.

Both groups of professionals continuously monitor customer preferences and oversee product development. They work closely with the manager of the business line or business unit to implement and carry out marketing and sales programs. All areas require they understand the product's function, its price, even its packaging and advertising. They know more about the product than almost anybody. This product pays their bills. They need to be expert communicators, whether they communicate by telephone, in a formal presentation, in a written proposal, or in casual conversation. Account executives and marketers depend on their ability to persuade.

At the higher level of sales and marketing hierarchy, you deal with a lot of information and communicate with a wide range of people. It is a fast paced environment. You must decide quickly, many times without enough information. Many people are uncomfortable working in this type of environment, but being first in the market is what it is all about. Meeting deadlines and sales goals make this a demanding career. These professionals travel a lot. They attend meetings and conferences to cultivate potential clients and other contacts. Communicating well and excellent interpersonal skills are indispensable. You are always selling and always trying to understand the changing marketplace. It is not enough to react quickly. You must anticipate. Create your future. This is not a profession to get into if you discourage easily or are tentative about making decisions. What other profession comes to mind that requires these same skills? When observing account executives and marketing professionals, many times it is difficult to tell where your work day ends and private life begins. The marketplace is not a nine to five environment.

Sales. Many people still think of store clerks and car salesmen. Or, maybe, a scene from Death of a Salesman pops into their heads. When I tell people I am in charge of sales for a couple of large accounts, I can tell they are thinking that what a shame it is I can't find a lawyer job. Actually, I'm making in the six figures, traveling to nice places, and driving a company car. I'm not that broken up about not practicing law.
            -Account executive for a large food service company

----

Account and marketing executives are near the top of the managerial hierarchy. As a group, sales and marketing people are some of the most highly paid people in this country. For a top, experienced marketing professional or account executive, your earning potential is unlimited. Bonuses may be multiples of your base salary. The more you make for your company, the more you make for yourself. You can move into these areas as either an account executive to some of the smaller accounts or, if the marketing side interests you, as a marketing assistant. Obviously, at these lower levels, the salary is not as lucrative as the account executive handling the larger accounts. However, opportunities for advancement to larger accounts and more responsibility abound if you prove yourself. Skill, energy, and enthusiasm get you into this career. Hard work and interpersonal skills make the business pay off.

Ads are the cave art of the twentieth century.
-Marshall McLuhan
(early-twentieth-century American psychologist
concerned about the effect of electronic media on children)

Public Relations

Public relations specialists gather information about their clients and present it to the public or customers truthfully, but also in the best light possible. They persuade without appearing to do so. Their work, in part, includes preparing statements on a client's accomplishments and activities. They may prepare statements for an officer of the company to read to the media or they may present it themselves. Many times, the work is very stressful because they are explaining an unpleasant occurrence, such as an environmental mishap or a factory accident. You have to be ready at any time to speak about life-threatening situations. Composure while communicating is the key. Most of the time, however, the news is not so serious, but still requires a bit of finesse. Financial reporting, especially whenever the news is not good, falls to the public relations spokesperson. He or she focuses the audience on the future while explaining lower than expected earnings.

Creativity, initiative, and interpersonal skills are important in this field. Many times, the hardest people to please are your clients. The press release you wrote says too much, or, maybe not enough. Everyone is critical, but, of course, no one else will write the release. You deal with chief executive officers, chief financial officers, senior management, and boards of directors. If you want exposure to people that can make a difference in the corporation, this is the career for you. You are their image and they will pay well for a good one.

Research skills serve you well. Background research helps you appear informed. Most press conferences will be full of questions. Some of the questions you will have expected; others will surprise you. The more background information and understanding you possess, the better you represent your client. Research skills honed in legal training apply to this career. Combine these research skills with your communications skills and experience and you offer a valuable package to prospective employers.

You must project a favorable image for your clients or employer any time you explain problems or policies. The more novel and persuasive you are, the more companies will pay you. You may find yourself in many different situations. This is especially true if you work for a public relations firm rather than a corporation. Your clients change every week. They may change every day. Special interest groups always need people with your skills. All of the leading edge companies have public relations people, either as employees or as consultants, representing them. They are on the leading edge of their business sectors and they want everyone, from customers to investors, to know it. Many times, you will be the persona of the company.

Although you are on call, most public relations people work a forty or fifty hour work week. Unfortunately, fighting a deadline, either television or newspaper, occurs more often than you would like. Many public relations people thrive on this type of pressure and feel this makes their job exciting. Some public relations professionals, especially those who represent large corporations, travel frequently to prepare statements on location at the corporations' far flung properties.

Jobs in business sector public relations occur either in consulting firms that specialize in public relations or the public relations departments of large corporations. Public relations spokespeople, like lawyers, must skillfully communicate in all types of media. The roles played by the public relations professional and the attorney are quite similar. Both of these professionals interface with a skeptical audience. The difference is the context. The public relations professional is in front of a camera; the attorney is in front of a jury. Legal training, with its emphasis on communication, is the best preparation for a career in public relations. Work experience will just make you better. Very few public relations professionals have college degrees in public relations. Most schools do not even offer such a curriculum. Most professionals have earned a degree in communications or journalism. They have learned most of what they know by doing it.

Some public relations firms and large international corporations have public relations staffs of more than one hundred professionals. These people usually specialize according to areas of expertise or geography. Most firms and corporations have much smaller staffs to handle public relations. The smaller the firm, the more likely it is that they will combine specialized tasks. No matter where you work, the better you are at handling challenging issues, the more value you add. The good public relations people thrive on this challenge. Some move on into the most challenging public relations career of all, politics.

I took some environmental courses in law school and they were pretty interesting. Interesting enough that I thought that was where I wanted to practice. It seemed, though, like half the graduating law students felt the same way.

A friend of the family suggested I try public relations emphasizing my knowledge of environmental law. He said many large companies have PR people that just handle their environmental problems and issues.

I ended up getting the first job I applied for. And, I really enjoy the work. I found out my real interest is with environmental issues; not just the law associated with them. I get to see a bigger picture.
-Public relations specialist with a
chemical manufacturing company

Although this book directs you to careers and opportunities in business, political careers sometimes grow out of these high profile business careers. Many politicians started as journalists or public relations professionals. Their experience with the media served them well. Be open to the opportunity if it interests you. If the past tells us anything about the future, it is not unheard of for a lawyer to get a good job in politics.

Work is much more fun than fun.
-Noel Coward
(early-twentieth-century English playwright and actor)

Manager of a Business Unit or Product Line

The business unit or product line managers are the consummate specialists/generalists, much like attorneys. Business unit managers are responsible for the operations of a particular division within the company. Divisions define themselves either geographically or by the product or products they produce. The product line manager is responsible for the results attributable to a line of products sold by the company. Whether you manage a business unit or a line of products, you are responsible for everything that happens in your particular area or product line, both good and bad. You choose the advertising, personnel, inventory; anything that is strategic to your area of responsibility.

You oversee all aspects of the business. You must effectively manage people. Successful managers, although taking responsibility for everything, do not do everything by themselves. They develop reliable teams. You may spend your day meeting with customers or suppliers or strategizing with your sales staff. You distill information and communicate it to the key members of your marketing, production, and sales teams. They help you successfully run the enterprise.

Because you deal with such a variety of situations and issues, your days have no routine. If you are a person who likes order and predictability in your job, forget about being a line or unit manager. The successful managers thrive on variety, unpredictability, and even chaos. The managers that bring order to chaos bring success to their enterprise and financial rewards to themselves.

The successful manager is always moving around. He or she needs to be out directing and helping the teams, not sitting behind a desk shuffling papers. A good manager spends time discussing, meeting, and presenting strategies. Getting out into the field to talk with salespeople and customers is extremely important. Legal training and experience provide invaluable communication skills. A unit manager or a line manager is primarily an oral communicator. The communication may take the form of a formal speech to senior management or an informal coaching session to teams of marketers and salespeople. Another skill honed by legal training is listening. The good manager listens to his or her staff, to customers, and to suppliers. It is this information, when used properly, that keeps the line or unit successful.

Balancing activities and managing time are major skills a business manager must have in order to be successful. Managers who cannot control their time do not last long anywhere. If they focus on minor problems they miss profitable opportunities. This does not mean that you do not pay close attention to your business, it just means that you delegate what you can and never view your work myopically. You have to set enough time aside to look at the big picture. Time management skills get honed in law school. The law student who cannot control his or her time will not last long either. The key skills for this position are leadership, communicating, and decision making. Successful attorneys need these very same skills.

I run a business within a business; three chain stores in a busy metropolitan area. It's as if they are my own. I've done everything over the past three years; negotiated with vendors, helped handle lawsuits, designed a local advertising campaign, and shoveled snow in the parking lot. I make pretty good money and have made some good friends. You never know what the week will bring.

            -Area manager for a retail merchandise chain

The business manager is responsible for every facet of the unit or product line: production, marketing, sales. He or she is like an owner of a small business. Business managers need to have both entrepreneurial skills, as well as intrapreneurial skills. As such, your services demand attention both from within and outside of the company. Terrific opportunities exist for managers to improve their market value. They can move laterally within the company. Business refers to this practice as cross-fertilizing. Competitors are always in the market for the managers of successful lines or units. It is also important to think globally. More companies are reaching into the foreign markets. The domestic business managers should view this situation as an opportunity for professional growth. A successful foreign assignment has put many business managers into senior level executive positions at relatively early ages. It is the new fast track. The financial rewards aside, you have the satisfaction of being in charge and running your own show. This career is for you if you like the idea of being in charge. This means when things go right, you get the credit, deserved or not. It also means that when things go wrong, you get the blame, deserved or not.

Human Resources Specialists

Successful companies realize that people make them successful. These companies need human resources professionals to bring in the best candidates and develop programs that motivate the work force to perform at a level necessary to compete in a worldwide economy. The effective human relations specialist is a strategic partner with the businesspeople. Being a strategic partner means understanding the business direction of the company. You know the goods and services your company produces. You know their capabilities and limitations. You are right in there with the front line people as opposed to playing the secondary administrative role of the old style personnel people.

Human resources specialists perform a variety of important tasks, including:

- playing a lead role in recruiting and selecting employees
- investigating employee complaints about the practices of the company or other employees
- communicating with employees on various company policies, procedures, and benefits
- assisting in designing compensation packages
- promoting the corporate image within and outside of the company

These tasks help define the job of the human resources specialist. Let us look at them more closely.

Recruiting and selecting employees. You screen applicants to find the right person and match that person with the open job. The search occurs either inside the company or outside, or both. Seeking a special type of employee always complicates the search. To effectively search, you must understand your company and its philosophy. In this way, you select the right individuals for the selection process. Only by understanding the full picture can you effectively screen the applicants before they interview at the department level.

Investigate employee complaints about the practices of the company or other employees. Human resources specialists involve themselves with the human element. This means dealing with such unpleasant situations as labor disputes, grievance proceedings, and terminations. Helping employees solve their workplace problems is your main task and is a worthy goal. Your legal experience and training afford you good listening and communication skills so that you can learn about and understand every side of the problem. Then, you distill the information down to a point so that you can act accordingly. Keeping in mind you must balance the needs of the company with the needs of the employee.

Sometimes, you have to make some difficult decisions, such as deciding the fate of an employee's livelihood. Your actions or those of your company may bring on some legal attacks by employees and former employees. Your knowledge of employment law and labor law will be invaluable in these unfortunate situations.

Communicate with employees on various company policies, procedures, and benefits. Human resources professionals communicate with employees, formally and informally, in written or oral form. People should be comfortable around you and trust you. Your legal training and experience have prepared you for this.

The size of the company you work for determines how general or specific your duties are. Your tasks are specialized in a larger organization. Larger organizations may have compensation specialists, benefits specialists, and pension specialists on staff to name a few. No matter what type of organization you choose, a background in labor law and employment law helps.

Assist in designing compensation packages. As competition increases, companies depend more on compensation and benefits programs closely connected with productivity. The human resources specialist creates compensation packages to match the profit goals of the corporation. These take the form of incentive bonus plans and profit sharing plans.

You look at this task from different perspectives. For many people, benefits for their family are their primary focus. You work on benefits for health care and child care. Many times these benefits retain the valued employees more so than extra money. By being creative here, you can help the employees and save your company money.

I was a solo practitioner for five years. I handled mostly employment cases: discrimination, wrongful firing, harassment. The hours were long and I really didn't put much money in my pocket after paying all my overhead. So, I'm putting my experience to work as a human resources manager. I know more than anybody in the group and feel confident, for the first time, about my future.

    -Ex-solo practitioner turned human resources specialist

Promote the corporate image within and outside of the company. You are on the road visiting with employees, communicating to a variety of people on subjects such as policy interpretation, compensation and benefits. You spend a lot of time resolving complaints. As you are doing all of these things, you represent the company. Organized, outgoing, and the consummate communicator describe you. This means listening to, and respecting the ideas of, the employees. Employees associate you with management and how management feels about its employees.

Entrepreneur

New opportunities for entrepreneurs are arising. The economy is responding to the high tech and service revolution. More individuals are changing careers and working for themselves. Major job growth will take place among small companies and millions of new start-up businesses. What does this mean for you?

If you do not find a career you like, create one! Build something of your own. The creating part is often more satisfying than the end result itself. Being an entrepreneur is as much a state of mind as anything else. Believing in oneself and the ability to make it on your own is the first step in any entrepreneurial venture.

However, do not be fooled. The entrepreneur's life is not always an easy one. Every venture requires capital. Many of these start-up ventures lose money at first. If you need a steady salary with benefits, entrepreneurship may not be the right path. Try to have some money to live on until the business gets going. This also means lowering your lifestyle. If you are unwilling to do this, I suggest you avoid working for yourself.

Raising capital occupies a great deal of time for most entrepreneurs. Entrepreneurs are always selling. It takes a lot of perseverance to succeed. You need to sell both your business concept and you. You must sell the financial community on your idea. You must sell customers on your product or service. You may even have to sell your spouse on the idea if the success rocket does not immediately take off.

Many times, you will have to put most of your net worth into your venture. You may find yourself asking family, friends, and business contacts to loan you money. In one sense it is best for entrepreneurs to provide as much of the initial capital as possible since by doing so they will own or keep most of the company. However, this makes the venture all the more risky. Many people cannot handle this type of risk. If you cannot, stay out of this career.

Muster all of your interpersonal and leadership skills you developed from your legal training. You will need them every day both inside and outside the company. Most entrepreneurs will tell you that technical knowledge is a distant second to being able to communicate with people and persuade them to do what you want them to do.

I bought and resold cars when I was in college. I had a T-shirt business in law school. The real reason I went to law school was because my dad and uncle were lawyers. Law school has really helped me. I am a lot more confident running my own business with my law background. But, running my own show is where I need to be. I like to make money and I like being in control. Win or lose.

-Owner of specialty catering business

Building something of your own is a source of immense satisfaction, not to mention wealth. Having more control over your time and your life is also a powerful motivation. The sky is the limit as to the type of business you get into. Just do your homework. Research here, just as in law, is crucial to success.

Once you get the business up and running, you will do all the things a big corporation does, such as human resources, operations, finance, and so forth. The difference is that you may perform all of these tasks yourself. At some point, hopefully, success will be yours and you will own a profitable, growing business. You will be able to delegate some of the things you do not like to do and just do the fun stuff. You will have more time for your family and have the time, as well as money, to do the things you have always wanted to do. You are at the end of the rainbow. The question becomes whether to cash out, and maybe, begin again, or take the business into its next phase. You could take your enterprise public with you at the helm. This option requires a more formalized business structure. There is also the issue of adding more staff. After the first ten million dollars or so, these kinds of problems or challenges are nice ones to have.

Property Manager

A characteristic of the boom and bust economy will be periods of rapid job growth and periods of stagnation or negative growth. Additional office building and retail properties will answer the demand and will still be there during the lull. These properties will need to be managed regardless of whether they remain at full capacity. Property management refers to financial and operations management of physical properties for the properties' owners. The property manager may be an employee of the owner or he or she may work for a property management firm that contracts out its services. Some businesses employ property managers to locate, purchase, and develop real estate for investment purposes or for use in the operations of the business. They also dispose of property suited to their uses. The firm earns a commission on the transaction.

A property management firm may service a variety of properties like apartments, shopping centers, and office buildings. Many property managers manage a mixed portfolio of different types of buildings. Some specialize in managing one type of property. Whether they specialize or not, the property manager is responsible for everything that goes on concerning the property. This means managing such routine items such as leasing, building maintenance, and so forth. In larger buildings, specialists handle such things as leasing, renovating, and subleasing. In smaller buildings, you perform all these functions. Your knowledge of contract law and property law make a lot of these tasks much easier. Employers recognize the value of a management professional who has a thorough understanding of these relevant areas. At times, you really will get to use your legal training. Lawsuits plague owners of large properties.

Property management ultimately is people management. A good manager is only as good as the people working in the building. Everyone has to work together and it is the job of the property manager to see that they do. When things do not work, or the service is inadequate, the property manager gets blamed. The tenants receive efficient and consistent service only when everyone connected with the property works together. You spend a lot of time making sure your workers know what to do and understanding and trying to comply with the tenants' demands. The communications skills of the lawyer come in handy here. You find yourself doing a lot of persuading.

People working with professional property management incline toward operating their own businesses. They enjoy performing a variety of functions each day. They enjoy working with people of varying abilities and personalities to solve problems on a routine basis. During normal business hours almost all of the tasks involve working with people. This means making telephone calls, conducting meetings, and walking around the building with a number of different individuals, including clients, tenants, and contractors. When the daily activities are over, you do all the paperwork associated with managing the property. This is not a nine to five job. It can be a twenty-four hour job if you allow it to be. If you are thinking about a career in property management, you must be honest about how involved you want to become in your job. Because property management is so similar to running one's own business, this job can become your life.

I am in charge of a ten story office complex. Everything is ultimately my responsibility. From making sure the toilets work to leasing arrangements with the tenants. I enjoy the work because there is a new challenge every day. Sometimes it's a twenty-four hour job. Other times it isn't quite as hectic. Contract law and property law, especially landlord and tenant, have really helped me. Property management is just a series of contracts.

-Commercial property manager in
the southwestern United States

Property managers often seek their first positions at institutions with property management departments—commercial banks, savings and loan associations, real estate investment trusts, government agencies, insurance companies, and mortgage brokerage firms. No matter where you go, the complex challenges require expertise and innovation. This makes property management a highly compensated profession.

Corporate Trainers

As our economy expands its service and high technology sector, so will employment. Intelligent workers with specific technical skills are the work force for the millennium. Workers have to continually develop new skills and competencies in order for their employers to remain competitive. The goal is to produce more productive, more highly motivated, and more responsible workers. Companies realize the importance of a well-trained work force and are willing to pay to have one. Creating effective workers requires training beyond that received in the typical education. In response, businesses must utilize the services of corporate trainers to devise and conduct programs for imparting these needed skills.

Corporate trainers either work for an individual company or they work for consulting firms specializing in training workers. No matter whether they come from the company or from the outside, their task is the same. They impart relevant skills on the client's work force. This takes a number of forms. They work with new employees to orient them to their jobs. They also introduce them to the policies and procedures of the company. The trainers provide all employees with the specialized skills needed for their jobs. Trainers often upgrade the skills of veteran workers by introducing new technologies and skills. Be prepared to teach a variety of skills. One week you might be reviewing the basics of mathematics for entry level workers. Next week you might conduct a word processing class for engineers. You must shift gears easily.

Trainers must first identify the needs of employers. Trainers use the following techniques, as well as a variety of others, to accomplish this task:

- questionnaires;
- interviews;
- job analysis; and
- aptitude tests

Trainers utilize the information received from these techniques and devise appropriate training programs. The employer desires a specific outcome from the training and it is up to the trainer to show how they intend to accomplish the desired result. You determine the program's content and decide on instructional methods and training materials to accomplish your assigned result. You can utilize a variety of techniques, such as role-playing, simulations, lectures, discussions, and demonstrations. Your personality and communication skills and the skill level and personality of your target class determine the type of program you select.

I was on the debating team in high school and college. I did all the courtroom competitions in law school. I enjoy talking in front of people. I guess I might be a little bit of a ham. And, I like to teach. I am too easygoing to be a litigator; it's not my nature. Being a

corporate trainer lets me do all those things I like without the adver-
sarial stuff. I teach all kinds of people different kinds of things. And,
quite frankly, it pays a lot more than teaching school.

-Corporate trainer for a business consulting firm

Corporate trainers work relatively normal work weeks. This is one of the few high-value careers having this characteristic. Your office is usually the offices or classrooms of your client company. Many larger corporate training firms have their own classroom facilities from where you will conduct your sessions. These facilities may include classrooms with networked computers or sophisticated audiovisual equipment.

Obviously, you have to be comfortable around people. You need excellent interpersonal skills and a knack for teaching. You must be the one that initiates the conversation and gets the ball rolling. This is not a job for introverts. You need every bit of tact and patience as you explain complex procedures or technical materials to a sometimes less than highly motivated audience.

After you have worked for a firm for a while, you may choose to work on a consulting basis for different corporations. If you take this route, you will need marketing, as well as teaching and communications skills. Conversely, after you have been a consulting trainer, you may find a company where you really enjoy working and that needs your services. Many experienced trainers find areas of expertise and specialize in them.

The measure of success is not whether you have a
tough problem to deal with, but whether it's the
same problem you had last year.
-John Foster Dulles
(attorney and secretary of state during the Eisenhower administration)

Management Consultants

Foreign competition is causing many American companies to examine the way they run their businesses. Gone are the days when inefficient businesses could maintain market share and earn a reasonable profit. Companies are turning increasingly to management consultants to address specific problems in reducing costs, streamlining operations, or maximizing business opportunities. Your client companies range from leading edge companies wanting to stay ahead of the pack to companies hanging on the financial ropes.

Consultants advise businesses how to run their companies. Management consultants do whatever helps a client's bottom line. There are a wide range of management consulting firms specializing in helping clients with certain problems and situations. Sometimes a consultant's work involves very short-term tactical tasks like helping to launch a new product. Other times, they stay with the company to see through their recommendations on a three-year plan.

Companies bring in outside consultants precisely because consultants are outsiders. They have experience looking at a wide range of companies. More importantly, however, it is often easier for consultants to sort through the organizational politics and solve the difficult problems. Many times, the client company's management knows the answer to the problem they have given to the consulting group. They want an outsider's opinion reinforcing their decision. Consultants ratify reorganization plans and associated downsizing.

Typically, consultants work in teams. The team leader breaks the problem into tasks, and each member of the team works on its task. The team begins by researching the problem. They determine the best approach to obtain the desired outcome. They estimate the time and staff the study will take. Once the plan gains approval from the client company, the teams begin analyzing the problem and begin developing possible solutions. The team collects information from client sources and external market research. They interview client personnel, customers, and suppliers. Consultants work with the company's management to analyze the problem and suggest solutions. Communications skills and people skills are necessary in developing clear and persuasive presentations setting out the best solution to the problem. The client reviews the plan and makes suggestions. Once the client feels comfortable with the plan of action, the consulting team implements the plan within the

company. Consultants often lead client task forces that are com-
missioned to implement the recommendations developed.

Consultants work in their own offices and also at their clients'
offices. The hours can be long, and extensive traveling to collect
data and talk with people frequently occurs. You need to love challenges to enjoy this job. The assignments challenge you constantly
in a variety of ways. Many times the challenges are stressful due to
deadlines and budget constraints. Successful consultants have
both analytical and interpersonal skills. The management consultant is a generalist/specialist much the same as an attorney.

---

*The truth is I did not graduate at the top of my law school class. In
fact, I was pretty close to the bottom. So, an attorney job was pretty
much out of the question. I ended up getting a job with the consulting
firm basically as a grunt. But, I really got into the work and they
promoted me. I guess I matured. Now, five years later, I have my
own accounts. I travel all over the country helping companies get
reorganized. Last year, my bonus put me over $100,000. It's funny
how things work out sometimes.*

-Account manager for an international
management consulting company

The most important task of the client and the consultant is insur-
ing a matchup between the consultant's area of expertise and the
problem at hand. The firm provides services on a contract basis,
commonly covering a specific project. Certain problems require
the resources of large firms. However, small firms handle other
problems, such as staffing and hiring issues, more adroitly than
large firms. The size of management consulting firms ranges from
the one person firm to large, international firms with hundreds of
employees. The large firms provide experience and training to
those coming into the business. The pay is quite lucrative, but the
hours are long. Management consultants run their businesses
much like law firms. They live on billing hours. If you are leaving
a firm because of the consuming work load, carefully investigate
the consulting firm's view of working hours.

Many attorneys have successfully started their own consulting firms. They usually focus on areas like communications, effective presentations, and team building within the client organization.

Education Consultants

Our demand for effective training to remain competitive in the global marketplace will exacerbate the shortcomings of the traditional public school system. The private sector will fill this void by providing innovative, computer-assisted teaching packages on a host of subjects. These packaged study programs will be for all levels of learning. They will include reading, mathematics, and science. The education consultant will also teach the more exotic subjects important to specialized groups. Entrepreneurial companies will form to provide these packaged programs and professional teacher consultants. Experienced teachers, computer applications specialists, and marketers will be among the founders because they recognize the need for their products and services. These companies will also provide the teachers themselves to teach selected groups of students willing to pay for the service.

These educational consulting firms will rely heavily on marketing to introduce their products and people into the educational stream of commerce. This is where people with communications and teaching skills add value. You will interface with teachers, parents, and the students themselves as you demonstrate your learning products or teach your chosen subject. Within ten years, the teaching products you market, and perhaps help design, will be commonplace.

My son was doing poorly in algebra. And, well, it was beyond me so I wasn't much help. He went to tutoring in the morning before school started, but he just wasn't getting it. A colleague of mine suggested a computer-assisted algebra course. I bought it, more out of desperation than anything else. It turned out to be one of the smartest things I've ever done. My son loved learning at his own speed on his own terms. He's not an A student, but he does a lot better. He uses the program to go over what he was exposed to in class. I'm sold on these packaged programs. They're not for everybody, but they might be for you.

-A once-exasperated father

Education consultants are the corporate trainers for those not working in large corporations. Your client base is people of all ages and backgrounds. Education consulting firms are forming with increasing frequency. Check with local schools and universities for the firms they utilize. The demand for their services is growing rapidly. These firms are looking for well educated people with innovative ideas. Some faculty members are already on the staffs of these firms. Visit with them about the kind of work the consulting group is doing. Ask them where the needs are in their school. See how you fit in. Be creative here. This area is in its infancy stages so the lines of communication develop slowly. This makes it difficult to find your way around, but it shows the field is in its early stages and explosive growth is ahead. This career suits both the entrepreneur and the intrapreneur.

I wanted to learn Spanish. I thought it would help me land a job in my company's international business development group. However, I didn't have the time to go to school at night to take classes. And besides, I had taken Spanish all through my school years and I remembered about three words. I came across this program put on by this firm specializing in teaching packages for the computer. I figured I would give it a try. The package was relatively cheap compared to what I would have spent on tuition or for private lessons.

I felt literate after a few lessons. I'm not, but I'm getting there. I can practice when I have the time, any time. The lessons are actually fun and they are practical. I believe in another month or two, I will have enough conversational skills to be comfortable with the language.

-Marketer for a Fortune 500 manufacturing company

Publishing

Research skills and good judgment are invaluable to the attorney. These same skills used in evaluating projects and manuscripts make editors successful. As with the attorney, the editor must write well. Publishing separates into two broad areas: book publishing and periodical publishing.

Book editors plan the line of books into which their publishing company invests money and staff. The publisher hopes to earn a suitable rate of return on its investment from the revenue received from sales of the book. Editors negotiate with the authors who submit manuscripts to the company. At issue are such things as royalties and future use of the material. Editors with legal training have an advantage in this area. As an editor, you are part of a team that evaluates hundreds of manuscripts looking for those very few that suit your purposes. "Will the book sell? What is the size of the readership?" are questions you must always be asking yourself.

Once you have decided to turn a manuscript into a book, you budget the project. You are an integral part of making the final product a reality. Along the way, you may ask the writer to revise his or her manuscript. Working with authors is sometimes not easy. Your interpersonal skills will help you here. Depending upon the type of publication, you may revise many of the manuscripts yourself.

Periodical editors work much the same as book editors. Periodical editors must always be sensitive to the demands of their subscribers. Lose your subscribers and you lose your livelihood. Topics must be timely and interesting. These topics, once selected, are assigned to staff and freelance writers. Once the author submits his or her work, the editor works with production people to make the article appealing to the readers. Tight deadlines sometimes make this work stressful. This is especially true in the newspaper publishing business. However, many editors say that it is these deadlines that bring out the creativity. As with book editors, periodical editors involve themselves in a lot of rewriting. They may do some writing of their own.

Whether you are in the periodical or book environment, strong writing and organizational skills are necessary. The same skills that helped you through law school will help you here. You need to be able to communicate with authors, your own staff, and, ultimately, to your readership.

Editors are open to many different topics. They are likely working with books or articles that cover a broad spectrum of subjects. Some editors concentrate on a single area of technical or professional interest, but even they must be generalists rather than specialists. Always remember, publishing is a business. Editors must have a strong business sense. They select the topics and projects and then keep them within the budget until they appear on the shelves. Successful projects bring on more successful projects and larger readerships.

I started into publishing while I was practicing law. I published a few short books of my own and found out I had a knack for it. I started publishing things for some other lawyers. Nonlawyers started coming to me after a while. It is a lot of work and I am not one of the big publishing houses. It's actually pretty much of a struggle, but it's getting better and I really like it. Maybe, when I get some time, I'll try writing that novel that is supposed to be in everyone.

-Attorney turned writer and publisher

An offshoot of publishing is writing. Many successful writers started out in some form of publishing. Some were copywriters. Some were reporters for magazines and newspapers. Patricia Cornwell, the wonderful mystery/suspense writer, who wrote thrillers like *Postmortem* and *Body of Evidence,* and the bestseller, *From Potter's Field,* did just that. She started out as a clerk and was later a police reporter for the *Charlotte Observer.* I know we are all happy she followed her dream to write.

If you are a lawyer or soon to be one and writing is your ambition, you do not have to go into publishing. Just start writing. Best-selling novelist, John Grisham, who authored *The Firm, The Pelican Brief,* and *A Time to Kill,* was a criminal defense attorney. The legal profession lost a fine attorney, but the world gained a wonderful writer.

*Writers aren't exactly people. They're a whole lot
of people trying to be one person.*
-F. Scott Fitzgerald
(early-twentieth-century American novelist)

Now It Is Up to You

These are high-value fields and careers. Undoubtedly there are others in both categories. Feel free to add them to the list. Remember, to effectively apply the strategy, you must:

- have a genuine interest in the fields and careers you selected; and
- show the skills developed from your legal training are effective for performing in these high-value careers.

This leads to the next part of the strategy.

Life is painting a picture, not doing a sum.
-Oliver Wendell Holmes, Sr.
(nineteenth-century-American physician and author)

Seeking the *Triple Point*

*We all live under the same sky, but we do not
all have the same horizon.*
-Konrad Adenaur
(Chancellor of Germany after World War II)

Merging Your Skills and Interests
into a *Triple Point*

Step Three of the strategy entails selecting one or more high-value career/high-value field combinations suited to your skills and interests. When you stop to think about it, a career is applying the skills and interests that a person has acquired over his or her lifetime to an economic endeavor. Your career identifies you. So, if it is going to define you, you should enjoy and be proud of what you do.

Step Three: Relate Your Skills to High-Value Careers

Identify high-value careers within high-value fields and relate your skills and interests to them. Most people spend more time planning a vacation than they do planning their career. Their careers just happen. That will not be the case with you. Spend some effort; this is your life. You have identified high-value fields and high-value careers. Now, select the ones that suit you and that you will enjoy. Remember Success Trait No. 1? Successful people love their work. They enjoy doing what they do. So, do not be tempted into taking the first job to come along. Once you start down the wrong career path, changing direction is difficult. You develop expertise in the wrong area. Moreover, this development is at the expense of developing expertise in a high-value career.

God gives every bird a worm, but
He does not throw it into the nest.
-Swedish proverb

Suppose you have narrowed down a few interesting high-value career/high-value field options. However, you really need to know a little more. Where do you go to find out more? There are several avenues open to you. You can try as many as you feel are necessary to become comfortable with your career choices. Every one of the high-profile careers and rapid-growth business sectors has several trade magazines and newsletters. Most are available at the public library. Libraries are good places to find various career books, business publications, and trade journals. Read through the articles and see if they interest you. If the articles do not hold your interest, this may not be the career or business sector for you.

Below is a partial listing of the periodicals available in the high-value fields and high-value careers. Be sure to read special issues that the trade publications publish. Read the year in review and forecast issues. You can get a cram course in the industry. Read companies you have targeted as being leading edge. Read about their competitors. It is a good idea to read basic business magazines and newspapers in addition to trade publications to get an overall feel for the business environment.

Organize yourself so that you can decide about your career quickly with the least amount of ambivalence. Do not worry if you find difficulty deciding among careers and fields. You can manage a job search in two or more avenues as long as you focus on a definite plan.

General Information on the Business Sector

Business Rankings Annual
Gale Research, Inc.
835 Penobscot Building
Detroit, MI 48226

Dun's Regional Business Directories
3 Sylvan Way
Parsippany, NJ 07054

Manufacturers' Directories
1633 Central Street
Evanston, IL 60201

Nation's Business
P.O. Box 51062
Boulder, CO 80323-1062

Standard & Poor's Services
25 Broadway
New York, NY 10004

High-Value Fields

Information Technology

Information Today
143 Old Marion Pike
Medford, NJ 08055-8750

PC Computing
P.O. Box 50253
Boulder, CO 80323-0253

PC Magazine
P.O. Box 51524
Boulder, CO 80323-1524

Telecommunications

Communications Quarterly
76 North Broadway
Hicksville, NY 11801

Telecommunications
685 Canton Street
Norwood, MA 02062

Telephone Industry Directory
Phillips Publishing
1201 Seven Locks Road
Suite 300
Potomac, MD 20854

Energy/Environmental

Environment
1319 Eighteenth St., NW
Washington, DC 20036-1802

*Environmental Industries
  Marketplace*
Gale Research, Inc.
835 Penobscot Building
Detroit, MI 48226

Independent Energy
PennWell Publications
P.O. Box 3105
Tulsa, OK 74101-3105

Oil & Gas Journal
PennWell Publishing
1421 South Sheridan Road
P.O. Box 1260
Tulsa, OK 74101

Power Engineering
PennWell Publishing
P.O. Box 1440
Tulsa, OK 74101

*USA Oil Industry
  Environmental Directory*
PennWell Publishing
P.O. 1260
Tulsa, OK 74101

World Oil
Gulf Publishing Company
P.O. Box 2608
Houston, TX 77252

Packaging Science

Food Engineering
One Chilton Way
Radnor, PA 19089

Food Processing
310 E. Erie Street
Chicago, IL 60611

Packaging Digest
P.O. Box 7568
Highlands Ranch, CO 80163-9368

World Wastes
P.O. Box 41369
Nashville, TN 37204-1094

Official Container Directory
Advanstar Communications
7500 Old Oak Blvd.
Cleveland, OH 44130

Biotechnology

R&D
P.O. Box 5800
Des Plains, IL 60017

*Research Technology
    Management*
Industrial Research Institute
The Sheridan Press
Fame Avenue
Hanover, PA 17331

The Biotechnology Directory
Stockton Press
49 West 24th Street
New York, NY 10010

Import/Export

Export Today
733 Fifteenth St. NW
Suite 1100
Washington, DC 20005

US Latin Trade
200 South Biscayne Blvd.
Suite 1150
Miami, FL 33131

Mexico Business
3033 Chimney Rock Road
Houston, TX 77056

High-Value Careers

Business Development

Forbes
P.O. Box 37159
Boone, IA 50037-2159

Fortune
Time, Inc.
Time & Life Building
Rockefeller Center
New York, NY 10020-1393

Harvard Business Review
P.O. Box 52621
Boulder, CO 80321-2621

Project Finance

Financial Analysts Journal
P.O. Box 3668
Charlottesville, VA 22903

Financial Executive
10 Madison Avenue
P.O. Box 1938
Morristown, NJ 07962-1938

Marketing/Account Executive

Potentials in Marketing
Lakewood Publications
50 South Ninth Street
Minneapolis, MN 55402

Selling
P.O. Box 7803
Riverton, NJ 08077

*Sales and Marketing
    Management*
355 Park Avenue South
New York, NY 10010

Public Relations

Public Relations Journal
33 Irving Place
New York, NY 10003-2376

Business Unit and Product Line Management

Advanced Management Journal
Society for Advancement of
    Management
126 Lee Avenue
Vinton, VA 24179

Management Review
American Management
    Association
P.O. Box 319
Saranac Lake, NY 12983

Human Resources

Employee Relations and
   Human Resources Bulletin
24 Rope Ferry Road
Waterford, CT 06386

HR Magazine
606 North Washington Street
Alexandria, VA 22314

Entrepreneur

Entrepreneur
P.O. Box 50368
Boulder, CO 80323-0368

Success
P.O. Box 3036
Harlan, IA 51593-2097

Inc.
P.O. Box 51534
Boulder, CO 80323-1534

Corporate Trainer

Training & Development
1640 King Street
P.O. Box 1443
Alexandria, VA 22313-1443

Training Magazine
50 South Ninth Street
Minneapolis, MN 55402

Property Management

Journal of Property
   Management
P.O. Box 109052
Chicago, IL 60610-9025

Professional Builder
8773 Ridgeline Blvd.
Highlands Ranch, CO 80126-2329

National Real Estate Investor
P.O. Box 1147
Skokie, IL 60076-9736

Real Estate Weekly
One Madison Avenue
New York, NY 10010

Education Consultants

Family PC
P.O. Box 37086
Boone, IA 50037-2086

Management Consultants

Dun's Consultant's Directory
3 Sylvan Way
Parsippany, NJ 07054

Sloan Management Review
P.O. Box 55255
Boulder, CO 80322-5255

Publication Editors

Publishers Directory
Gale Research, Inc.
835 Penobscot Building
Detroit, MI 48226

Publishers Weekly
P.O. Box 6457
Torrance, CA 90504-9806

Read these publications creatively. Notice how people in the field and the career succeed. What characterizes them? Study the stories to see how you might add value. Work at this. The more you know about the company, the more you can relate your skills and background to a company's needs. You will be glad ten years from now that you took this time to do this.

If you are currently unemployed, be particularly careful when assessing new jobs or careers. Low self-esteem often causes you to look at less challenging careers more readily than you normally would. A common mistake is to decide based only on criterion: *Will they hire me?* Again, the day will come that you will be glad you had a plan of action and stuck with it.

I spent a solid month in the library researching the computer business. The library was my office. I read everything I could. Annual reports, Standard & Poor's, trade magazines, anything and everything. I knew a lot, a whole lot. I knew the companies where I wanted to work at and the ones I didn't. I know some people thought I should be out looking or sending resumés or something. You know, looking for a job. But, when I applied to the companies, I knew just what to write in my resumé and what to talk about at the interview. I got a job and my friends were still looking.

-Account executive for a software company

What have you done so far? You have identified the high-value fields and careers. Then, you matched your skills and interests to target a career or careers within the field or fields. Now, you need to determine the *leading edge companies* within the high-value field. A *leading edge company* is a company that innovatively leads, or is close to leading, its high-value business sector. These are the companies that you want to contact. This is the *triple point*. This is your goal. A triple point is a high-value career in a high-value field with a leading edge company. This is Step Four.

Step Four: Target the *Triple Points*

Target the *triple points:* A high-value career in a high-value field with a leading edge company.

> *No wind favors him who has no destined port.*
> -Michael DeMontaigne
> (sixteenth-century French essayist)

Finding Leading Edge Companies

No one can guarantee the future. However, you can maximize your career opportunity by analyzing your potential employer within its industry. Understand its business posture and its future outlook. You can do all this by analyzing the same information that you looked at when you studied the high-profile fields. The articles will mention the prominent companies frequently. Some may be leading edge companies; others may be dinosaurs waiting to die. How do you know which companies are leading edge companies? You can figure this out asking these questions:

- Which companies seem to lead the pack in innovation?
- Which companies are always in the news?
- Which companies have strong earnings?

- Which companies are expanding? Is the expansion into new geographic markets or into new product lines?
- How do the companies seem to differentiate themselves from the others in the field?

This is a critical step. Your future happiness and success are inseparable from the company's current strategy and competitive position in the marketplace and in the future trends of the industry. You may be a great employee, but if the company files for bankruptcy, your career hits the skids.

Section C of the Appendix contains worksheets with the preceding questions so that you can organize your search. Once you find an interesting field, go through these questions and determine the leading edge companies in the field. Notice there are a few identical sets of these questions. This accommodates the fact that more than one field may interest you. Identify leading edge companies in each of the fields of interest.

I worked hard for ten years and have nothing to show for it. I worked for two companies during that time and both went belly up. I'm never going to work for anybody unless I feel good about their financial condition and their future. I learned the hard way.

                          -Ex-employee of bankrupt firms

One Final Place to Look

You have done all the research you can. However, you are still not sure. At this juncture, find professionals in the area of interest and ask them about their jobs. People love to talk about themselves. Trade and professional associations are great sources of *unofficial* information. You can realize a different perspective by speaking with people in these associations. You can attend luncheon or dinner meetings hosted by the professional organization and painlessly accomplish your mission. You can mingle at the cocktail hour and find out what the career or the business sector that interests you is really like. I call this *informational interviewing*. Some think it is the best way to assess careers. Asking the right people about careers in certain industries and the prominent companies in it is a good way to add to your knowledge base. More importantly, it avoids the common situation of many unhappy workers who are now saying—"If I had only known then, what I know now."

I went to an energy trade show just to look around. I thought I might have wasted my money because the admission was seventy-five dollars. That seventy-five bucks was the best investment I ever made! I got all the information I needed in about two hours because it was all in one place and they were giving it away. They wanted you to have it. I got names of people to contact. I struck up a conversation with an account rep. She mentioned her company might be expanding into the Northeast. Well, I am from there and wanted to go back. My cover letter and resumé were right on target.

-Successful job seeker, now employed in Boston

This is your new idea. Keep leveraging yourself—high-growth career, rapid-growth business sector, and a rapidly growing company within the sector. In so doing, your career will grow geometrically, as opposed to the average worker who, at best, is just staying even to where he or she was last year. This is why you aim your efforts at these targets.

Hitting the Target

You are after a successful career, not a summer job. You must be willing to innovate and be creative. The old approaches simply are no longer effective. We have selected the targets. The next step is to build, guide, and land a powerful, job-seeking missile into the target. Then, as a result, you will get the opportunity to sell yourself at an interview with your target employer. So, let's get to it.

To do great and important tasks, two things are necessary:
a plan and not quite enough time.
-Anonymous

Chapter Seven

Making Contact

Wealth is the product of man's capacity to think.
-Ayn Rand
(twentieth-century Russia-born American novelist)

You're in Business Now

Legal training is comprehensive and intensive so it applies to a wide variety of career disciplines. You are preparing for some exciting and lucrative careers, careers that do not fall under the rubric of practicing law. This is your design. Businesses need people with certain backgrounds in various strategic positions. At least one-quarter of the law school graduates do not practice law; hardly any would leave their lucrative business careers to do so.

Begin thinking like a business person. Describe your skills, background, and experience in business terms. Adopt the buyers' background. If you force the business community to translate its needs to your legal training, they will not view it as worth their time. They will move on to other candidates.

Many of the job hunting strategies that you grew up with fail in today's rapidly changing economy. They worked years ago, but they do not now; too much has changed. The growing dynamic companies want specifically skilled, mature, motivated people that are ready to go to work and make them money. Gone are the big bureaucratic and benevolent companies with one-year training programs looking for people with certain grades or number of years of experience at a job. Today, you must add value immediately.

You Are Selling You

The employer is buying. Always think in terms of how you can *add value to the employer.* It is that simple. It even sounds a little crass. However, this is the context. Sell your background and skills to a target employer in business terms. How do you do this? Well, any time you want to sell something, anything, you must:

- introduce the product, whatever it is, to the buyer,
- describe the product concisely, and
- sell the product in a clever and interesting way by presenting facts about the product that interest the *buyer.*

> *If the only tool you have is a hammer, you*
> *tend to see every problem as a nail.*
> -Abraham Mallow
> (early-twentieth-century American psychologist)

Dust Off That Resumé? Not Just Yet

So what is your first inclination? Most people respond by writing a resumé, usually the one-page type. I am sure you are familiar with the type of resumé I am talking about. They are very general so that they can be mass mailed. Not to mention that they usually read like an obituary notice. These mass mail out resumés do not meet any of the selling criteria because they:

- are short without being concise,
- are dull and do not interest the buyer,
- are trite and banal rather than interesting and informative, and

- generalize about only what interests the seller, rather than state particulars that interest the buyer.

The last bullet is the most glaring shortcoming. In order to sell yourself, you must show what you can and will do for the buyer/employer.

I get about ten resumés a day; day in and day out. And, they all seem to be the same. One page long; list of jobs since the applicant was eighteen; vague employment objectives; and list of hobbies. I think there is only one resumé and people just put their name and address on it. I don't read them. At the most, I skim them. Each gets date stamped and put in a file. When the files get too big, we throw them away. Not a great way to ask for a job. I guess the positive thing is that the writer didn't waste much time writing it.

-Human resources manager for
a medium-size corporation

Focus on What You Will Do

A resumé's major shortcoming is it mainly addresses what the seller *wants*, rather than what the seller will *do*. There are thousands of books written on how to write resumés. They elevate writing and mailing out resumés to a science. Job seekers continue to use them as their main tool although employers, and the job hunters themselves, know they do not work very well. Large companies receive close to one million resumés each year and now use resumé scanning software to handle the flurry of resumés. Resumés were more effective when it was a sellers' market. However, downsizing has turned this around. Yet, few are reluctant to change their approach.

Am I suggesting you should not draft a resumé? Quite the contrary. Your resumé is still important to your job search. You should take great care to write an effective one. They are important and I have devoted the last half of this chapter to helping you write an effective resumé. However, I do not want it to be your primary selling tool. The introduction letter should be. Here is why.

Introduction Letters as Superior Selling Tools

Contact your *triple point* target with an introduction letter accompanied by a resumé. Let the introduction letter be your first contact with the potential employer. The letter is your first impression. Make it a good one because you will not get a second chance. Showcase and translate your legal training into skills needed to perform the high-profile position. Make the points you need to make and eliminate those canned objectives readers skim over. No one really cares what you did five summers ago, what your hobbies are, or the names of your children. Do not make the reader strain to figure out what it is that you will actually do.

Thoughtfully written introduction letters focus on the following three points:

- the important relevant things that you have done,
- the relevant skills you have, and, most importantly,
- what you will do for the employer in terms of adding value.

Step Five: Contact Your Triple Point Target

Contact your triple point target with an introduction letter accompanied by a resumé. The introduction letter sells. It is your thirty-second advertisement. These letters must be energetic, enthusiastic, and, of course, realistic. Set out your special skills to the employer:

- the ability to communicate,
- self directed,

- a leader and a team player,
- persuasive,
- critical thinking, and
- legal knowledge relevant to business.

The introduction letter must show that a person in control of his or her destiny wrote it, the kind of employee the employer wants in his organization. Remember, up to this point, nothing is more important than the letter. A targeted, well-written introduction letter greatly increases your chances of getting to the interview phase.

How to Go About It

You've already researched about ten to fifteen companies. They are part of your triple points. You should keep current information about them handy. Now you are ready to start making contact. Here is the process, in a nutshell:

- Focus your research to determine how you can add value to the company.
- Ascertain the person who actually hires in the target company. This means the department head and not just someone in the human relations department.
- Craft an introduction letter showcasing your legal training skills in terms of the business sector. Point out what you can and will do for that person.
- Enclose a resumé that complements the introduction letter.
- Follow up, by telephone, to that person on a prearranged date.

Section D of the Appendix contains introduction letter and resumé writing worksheets. The worksheets ask for certain specific information about the target company and you. By having this kind of specific information in front of you, you will be able to effectively target your introduction letter and resumé. Finish reading through this chapter so that you can get a good idea of how to write your introduction letters and resumés. It is up to you if you want to utilize the worksheets or create a system of your own. The goal is to have the relevant, specific information collected and distilled into a coherent, usable form. For further discussion on this important facet of the career search, refer to the further suggested readings in Section E of the Appendix.

Research Is the Key—Just Like Law School

Let's look at the first bullet above. Too many people do not realize how many ways research helps them find a job. It is much more than just compiling a list of business names and addresses or reading articles about a company before an interview. Research can assist you in every step of your job hunt. If you have done it right, you will be able to write a more targeted introduction letter and resumé because you know the dynamics and needs of the company, as well as what the high-profile career generally requires. You waste time if you highlight strengths and experiences that are of no interest to the company. Research uncovers key information for you to bring up during the interview. Employers want people familiar with the business. You have got the advantage here because research was a way of life in law school. Just apply yourself a little differently now.

They are able who think they are able.
-Virgil
(Roman poet)

Determining the target company's needs is the most difficult step in the research process. Consequently, most people skip it. Why? Because it requires thoughtful work. It also means that you cannot write a generic introduction letter and resumé to mail out to hundreds of potential employers. This is vestigial thinking from the old resumé mail out days. Sure, you get them out fast, but they do not do the job. Make the effort count.

Step Six: Define Your Career Selection

Define your career selection in terms of your legal training and experience. You have gotten all the information you need. Find out to whom you should send the letter and resumé. Always address the introduction letter to a person. Preferably, the person who does the hiring. *Dear Sir/Madam* or *To Whom It May Concern* greetings are so unprofessional I will not even talk about them. Do you read those kinds of letters? Why would you expect others to?

Many times the research article will contain the name of the contact person. Other times, you will have to call the target company and find out whom to contact. Some job applicants do not like to do this. It embarrasses them. If it makes you feel better, imagine you are a potential customer and you want to get hold of someone in the company. Call with that mind-set or attitude and it will be a lot easier. Once you have gotten a contact name, you are ready to craft the introduction letter.

Form and Function

Good form is just common sense. Think about the form of a letter that would impress you. Let me suggest the following to give you a professional looking introduction letter:

- Always utilize high quality bond paper and envelopes. Make it look like you are the person of value that you are. As stated earlier, always send the letter to a person.
- Use the active voice and write in the first person. *You* are communicating to another *person.*
- Use business-like language, but not to the point of being impersonal. Avoid jargon and any annoying industry buzzwords.
- Be yourself by finding your own voice. Employers want real employees, not clones. That is why mass produced generic resumés do not work.
- Watch your language and grammar. Remember, the reader will use the whole letter to evaluate you.

Spend time on your letters. Rewrite and edit numerous times. When you think it is perfect, have someone else read it. Maybe it is not so perfect. Because letters are personal, they invite reading. People read letters, but they scan resumés.

Begin by specifically stating the purpose of the introduction letter. That is why you want to know about the person to whom you are writing and as much as you can about the job you are seeking. The opening must get their attention. You get their attention by talking about what specifically interests them. Writing to Dear Sir/ Madam and asking if there are any job openings will get your letter date stamped and filed, but not read. Talk to the reader when you write. Sell yourself, but avoid wild, unsubstantiated claims.

Follow the purpose with your qualifications. Relate two to three aspects of your work experience and legal training to the job. Build your letter around these main points. Tailor each letter to the job by adding specifics. However, the meat of the letter that sets out your qualifications and accomplishments should remain unchanged from letter to letter. In order to come up with your *applicable* strongest points, ask yourself:

- Does this example show how much I could contribute to the company?
- Are there concrete facts that I can use to back up my claim?
- Is this claim specific? Is it important to the company?
- Is this skill or quality central to the job I am trying to get?

Think like a businessperson when writing. First, show the buyer that a need exists. Then, you fill that need. Obviously, this is more challenging to do when you are changing careers or you have little experience, as is the case with many new graduates. This means you will have to draw parallels with the experience you have. Your experience may be limited to just your law school experience. Concentrate on skills and experiences that sell you best. Work with what you have. The career path is a continuum; you do not have to start at the highest point. That would be nice to do, but that is not a reasonable expectation.

The beauty of the introduction letter is that it focuses on what is important to the employer. Superfluous facts, irrelevant summer jobs, and vague career objectives distract the reader. This focus should carry through to the resumé.

Focus Exclusively on Skills and Experience That Add Value. Resist Filler.

Wind up your letter as positively as you opened it. Restate in one or two sentences what you will do for the company. Close the letter stating you will follow up by telephone on a certain date to make an appointment. You take the initiative by stating a definite time that you will call. Do not finesse this issue. You want a job. You are making it clear that you can contribute and both of you will benefit.

> *All the genius I have is the fruit of labor.*
> -Alexander Hamilton

I read every cover letter I receive, the good ones and the bad ones. It doesn't take long and the letter tells you more about the person than the resumé. Letters are personal. Resumés are cookbook. The cover letter tells how badly the applicant wants the job by how much effort they put into the letter. If they work hard to get the job, they will work hard when they have the job. The resumé? I only read the resumé on the day the applicant comes in for an interview.

-Vice president of marketing for
an import-export company

Here is an example of an introduction letter written to a leading edge company in the computer software business. The writer recently graduated and a career in public relations interests her:

ELLEN LEGALEAGLE
123 Main Street
Law City, NY 11202
(212) 765-4321

September 1, 1997

Ms. Mary Employer
Director of Public Relations
Leading Edge Company
1 World Plaza
Business City, NY 11000

Dear Ms. Employer:

May I help you as an associate public relations specialist?

I want to put my communications skills to work. I have recently completed law school course work designed to further develop my skills for a career in business. I participated in mock trial and moot court competitions throughout my entire law school career. In so doing, I have experienced representing a client to the public, both in the printed and spoken media, under the most adverse circumstances. My training included having experienced attorneys and actors coach me on improving my presentations and rapport with juries, clients, and audiences. Developing rapport is the essence of lawyering, and I want to bring this into my public relations career.

My formalized training includes business related courses giving me a solid foundation in contracts, agency and partnership, labor law, intellectual property, business organization, and employment law. I can relate to the issues that Leading Edge Company encounters conducting business because I have studied business from the issues confrontation perspective. This background understanding lets me think on my feet a little easier than most people in the field.

I want to be part of a ground-breaking software company. Your recent development of the XYZ software is quite exciting and puts Leading Edge ahead of its closest competitors, Alpha Corporation and Beta Company. The next step of informing and selling the public will be critical to your success. I can assist you in this important area.

I have enclosed my resumé providing additional information. I will contact you, by telephone, on September 21 to discuss your interest.

Best regards,

Ellen Legaleagle

Let us use this first introduction letter as a guide.

- Notice, first of all, that the introduction letter specifically mentions a job area—associate public relations specialist. Mary Employer does not have to guess what type of work Ellen wants to do.
- Ellen specifically relates two of her strong points, communications skills and business structure knowledge, to the public relations job. She explains why these are attributes to a career in public relations and how she attained these skills through law school course work.
- She states she wants to work for Leading Edge because it is an innovative leader in the business. She keeps this from being an empty statement by citing their ground-breaking software.
- She shows her knowledge of the business by mentioning the XYZ software and Leading Edge's two competitors.
- She creates a need—informing and selling the public on XYZ software—and offers to fill that need.
- Ellen closes with a date on which she will contact Mary. This tells Mary that Ellen is serious enough about the job to take action.
- She encloses a resumé to complement the introduction letter.
- Notice the overall positive and professional tone of the letter.

*The quality of a person's life is in direct proportion
to their commitment to excellence, regardless of their
chosen field of endeavor.*
-Vince Lombardi
(professional football coach and ex-law student)

An attorney wanting to exit the legal business and move into the human resources side for an energy company crafted the following introduction letter:

JOHN LEGALEAGLE
123 Main Street
Law City, NY 11202
(212) 765-4321

September 1, 1997

Mr. John Employer
Leading Energy Corporation
2 World Plaza
Business City, NY 11000

Dear Mr. Employer:

Are you in need of a human resources specialist able to deal with the difficult problems facing companies as employers?

Practicing law for ten years has exposed me to a variety of labor and employment issues, including job discrimination and sexual harassment claims. Now I would like to put my experience to work for you. I can recognize and deal with these problem situations early on before they become adversarial. Early action prevents yesterday's predictable situations from becoming today's problems and tomorrow's lawsuits and unfavorable publicity. The most looming example of such a problem situation is the issue of wrongful firing. Primary Energy Corporation is being sued in this area by a former employee. My sources tell me that they will not be alone in this arena. I can head off problems such as these because I have been on the other side and know how to prevent these unfortunate situations from occurring. I spent two years of private practice interviewing former employees and their employers and subsequently developing strategies to represent former employees. The vast majority of the cases followed similar patterns yielding predictable consequences.

I want to work for a company that is creating its own future such as Leading Energy is. Your energy swap transactions have made you a leader in the energy business. As your work becomes more complex, your employee needs will follow suit. Unfortunately, so do some problems. If you want to be ready for the future in the human resources area, in the same way as you are in the energy area, I would like to talk with you.

I have enclosed my resumé providing additional information on my training and experience. I will follow up by phone on September 21 and see if there is a mutual interest.

Sincerely,

John Legaleagle

Examine John's introduction letter. Notice the similarities in the two introduction letters even though:

- John has different skills and experience than Mary, and
- he is seeking a different career in a different field from Mary.

John identifies early on the job he is seeking. He mentions that he has specific experience in the human relations area and explains how his experience directly translates to what Leading Energy needs. John indicates his knowledge of the business by mentioning the energy swap transaction, showing that he will successfully move from lawyer to businessperson.

He creates a need: head-off employment problems. He specifically mentions such a problem is besetting Leading Energy's competitor, First Energy. He answers the need because he was on the other side and knows what to do and what to avoid. John closes with a follow-up contact date. Again, this shows interest and self-direction.

> *Genius is one percent inspiration and*
> *ninety-nine percent perspiration.*
> -Thomas Edison

Most graduates do not know how to look for a job. They do not put the effort into the process that's needed. It's not taught in school. And many of these Get-a-Job-Quick books make it sound like a few magic words is all you need. It's as if everybody worries about getting a job, but nobody does anything about it. We're not miracle workers They need to do some work.

> -Partner in a professional recruiting firm

Here is a sample of a recent graduate seeking a job as a marketer in the food packaging industry. Karen has very little job experience except for working as a sales clerk in a clothing store.

KAREN NEWEAGLE
123 MAIN STREET
LAW CITY, NY 11202
(212) 765-4321

September 1, 1997

Ms. Mary Employer
Vice President of Marketing
Leading Packaging Corporation
3 World Plaza
Business City, NY 11000

Dear Ms. Employer:

May I be of help to you in an entry level capacity in marketing Leading Packaging's new line of frozen food packaging?

Selling; whether it is a position or a product, is the essence of my training and experience. I recently graduated from law school where I won several mock trial advocacy awards. I was also quite successful on my college debate team. In both activities, I have benefited from the coaching of practicing attorneys and actors to learn how to effectively make a point. I have spent a lot of hours and worked hard to make it look easy. Now, I want to use my skills to help your marketing effort. I want to be out in front where all the action is.

I am familiar with introducing new product lines. I was a sales associate in an upscale clothing store. New product lines are synonymous with the fashion industry. I learned first hand how new lines are tested and then brought in. This is where I developed my interest in marketing new product lines.

I realize the goal of marketers is to get the customer to sign a contract. My law school course work included intensive course work in contracts. I have an added advantage in that I have seen what makes good contracts, as well as bad ones. I have learned from the expertise and misfortune of others. My training has also given me a solid grounding in the structuring of business organizations, such as partnerships, joint ventures and corporations. Leading Packaging routinely deals with all of these business structures.

I want to take my energy and skills to a company that displays similar high energy and innovation. Leading Packaging is certainly at the top of the list as it posts the highest return on assets of all the packaging firms. The new frozen food packaging line will help Leading Packaging stay ahead of your competitors. I can help that happen.

I have enclosed my resumé providing additional information on my background and training. I will follow up by telephone on September 21 that we may talk further.

Best regards,

Karen Neweagle

Karen's letter takes a slightly different approach, but the basic concepts are there.

- She begins by specifically stating the job that interests her— entry level marketer. She uses the new product line as a vehicle to do this. In doing so, she shows she knows about Leading Packaging and the importance of its new product line.
- Karen highlights her communications skills and business course work and relates them to the marketing job. She ties in her limited experience as a clothing store sales clerk to the target job.
- She closes by expressing an interest to work for Leading Packaging and shows she has researched their performance relative to the rest of the packaging industry.
- She lets Mary know that she will call her in a few weeks. This shows her interest and self-motivation.

Notice how all three introduction letters translate the legal experience into business expertise. You need to do this for the reader. Do not assume the employer knows what legal training entails. Translating is critical to your success. All three writers had differing levels of actual job experience. All three will probably enter at different points on their career paths of interest. But no matter what their level, they all specifically tied their experience to the jobs they are now targeting.

Look at this sample introduction letter from a recent graduate seeking a job as a corporate trainer. William does not have any work-related experience. So, he can only utilize his law school experience to showcase his skills.

WILLIAM LEGALEAGLE

123 Main Street
Law City, NY 11202
(212) 765-4321

September 1, 1997

Ms. Samantha Employer
Head Corporate Trainer
Universal Manufacturing Corporation
3 World Plaza
Business City, NY 11000

Dear Ms. Employer:

Are you in need of an assistant corporate trainer in light of Universal's recent expansion into the communications equipment manufacturing sector?

I want to put the communications and teaching skills I have developed in law school to work as a corporate trainer. I have recently completed my law school course work in which I concentrated on communicating difficult, and sometimes controversial, ideas to groups of people. Mock trial and moot court participation and various clinic courses in trial advocacy, client counseling, and negotiations seminars have given me the benefit of the experience of practicing attorneys to improve my presentations. This intense training regime developed my communication and organization skills needed to effectively train employees in new skills.

My training also emphasized research and writing skills designed to effectively discuss and persuade through clear and concise writing. My writing project was a fifty-page paper requiring hours of research, and many further hours, to distill the information into informative and persuasive writing. Most of this research was computer-assisted so I have a working knowledge of computers I can demonstrate to others.

Universal has timed its expansion well to take advantage of the exploding growth in the communications sector. In order to capitalize on this expansion, your group will have to train and motivate the work force. I would like to help with that endeavor and believe I can assist your group.

I have enclosed my resumé setting out additional information regarding my background and training. I will contact you, by telephone, on September 21 to discuss this further.

Best regards,

William Legaleagle

William's introduction letter effectively shows that he is aware of Universal's activities by citing their expansion into communications equipment manufacturing. This shows Samantha that William has made an effort to understand Universal's business. William creates, and then offers to fill, the need for training the work force to handle the expansion into communications equipment manufacturing. He cites the skills needed to be a successful corporate trainer. He explains how he acquired these skills in law school.

William's situation is very common. He is a law school graduate with little or no work experience. He does a good job making his law school experience fit the entry level corporate trainer position requirements.

Katherine, the next job seeker, is an attorney with a few years of solid work experience. She wants to change fields into management consulting. She starts with the following introduction letter.

KATHERINE LEGALEAGLE
123 Main Street
Law City, NY 11000
(212) 765-4321

September 1, 1997

Mr. Robert Employer
Stamford Business Consultants
6 World Plaza
Business City, NY 11000

Dear Mr. Employer:

I want to apply my business skills and experience as an account executive for a consulting firm having a client base of fast moving, innovative companies.

I have been an associate corporate counsel for a medium size specialty steel products manufacturing firm for the past two years. I have been part of the negotiating teams involved with sales contracts of specialty pressurized steel containers both to domestic and international customers. The total value of these sales contracts was on the order of $10 million. On the other side, I have negotiated supply contracts with vendors for raw materials for feedstock in the steel-making process and for natural gas as fuel for the manufacturing plant. In so doing, I have become familiar with the manufacturing operations and financials. My interests, as a result of participating in these projects, have shifted into a broader business range. I believe my manufacturing experience will make me an asset to your consulting group.

Your consulting firm interests me because of your work with specialty mills, in particular with those that are exporting their products. I understand that your team helped American Specialty Steel Company land a large order with an Australian-based petroleum refiner in the process of expanding. My international experience includes working with Asian and southeastern European customers. I was on a project team responsible for a $5 million sale of specialty steel goods to Pakistan. Prior to that, I was on the team working on a turnkey arrangement to fabricate a specialty mini-mill in Thailand. I want to make the change into the consulting area where I can use my experience and add upon it.

I have enclosed my resumé setting forth additional information on my background and experience. I will contact you by telephone on September 21 to discuss any mutual interest.

Best regards,

Katherine Legaleagle

Notice how Katherine used specifics to describe her work experience. She used dollar amounts and mentioned the specific types of contracts and customers. This type of specificity helps the reader translate legal experience to business experience. Specificity helps Robert relate to Katherine. Again, we see the importance of research. Katherine's research told her about the American Specialty Steel situation. Robert knows Katherine is aware of what is going on in the business.

A recent graduate with no work experience wrote the following introduction letter. The growing private sector education field interests Mark. He introduces himself to the owner of a newly created company that creates, packages, and sells educational materials and courses.

MARK LEGALEAGLE
123 MAIN STREET
LAW CITY, NY 11202
(212) 765-4321

September 1, 1997

Ms. Susan Employer
President
NewMethod Educational Systems
8 World Plaza
Business City, NY 11000

Dear Ms. Employer:

I want to be part of your company's growth by designing and marketing packaged educational materials.

My undergraduate and law school coursework required successfully communicating my ideas. Legal training stresses the importance of precise and persuasive written and oral communication. Being a part of your company's efforts to develop innovative educational courses is exciting. I enjoy designing creative ways to teach and communicate with others.

In law school, I observed that some students found group study effective—others found that they needed to develop their own learning programs. Just as an attorney needs to target his arguments to persuade the jury, so one needs to tailor one's teaching methods to the student. Your individualized packaged reading and math programs are an excellent example of doing just that.

Because law school requires a lot of writing, faculty experienced and trained in effective communication train us to be effective writers. I want to use this training and experience to help others improve their writing skills. I feel I can contribute to your company's work in this area.

I have enclosed my resumé setting forth additional information on my training and background. I will contact you, by telephone, on September 21 to see if we might discuss my ideas further.

Best regards,

Mark Legaleagle

Mark does several things well in his introduction letter. He relates his law school experience in terms of learning, something that obviously interests Susan. He mentions NewMethod's products on different occasions showing that he is aware of what the company is doing. Mark does more than ask for a job. He informs Susan that he has an idea regarding teaching writing that he would like to discuss with her. This shows Susan, whether she is interested in this particular topic or not, that Mark and she are thinking along the same lines. Susan should be confident that Mark will be able to contribute immediately. Small, entrepreneurial companies do not have the time or personnel to set up training programs.

Here is one last sample of an introduction letter. Frank is a practicing attorney with quite a bit of work experience. He is seeking a business development position in the import/export sector.

FRANK BEENANEAGLE
123 MAIN STREET
LAW CITY, NY 11202
(212) 765-4321

September 1, 1997

Ms. Joan Employer
Vice President of Marketing
Leading Import-Export Company
4 World Plaza
Business City, NY 11000

Dear Ms. Employer:

Do you need a business development professional with several years of international experience?

I have practiced law in the international arena for the past five years. I have negotiated and drafted partnership and joint venture agreements with industry partners from Central America and South America. I am particularly proud of a $30 million joint venture project in Argentina that I helped get back on track after the parties had closed off their discussions. This sense of accomplishment resulting from successful facilitating and negotiating is now what I am seeking. Business development is where I want to focus my interest and expertise.

I want to work for Leading because of its commitment to developing the Central American and South American markets. Your recent contract to supply oilfield equipment to Pemex leaves you well positioned for further work in Mexico and Central America. I can help develop those markets for you. I am fluent in both spoken and written Spanish. I have worked with Pemex on several occasions. Most recently I worked on a $10 million sales contract involving specially fabricated oilfield production equipment. This contract was one of the first such arrangements consummated in Mexico. I would like to give Leading the benefit of my experience and expertise.

I have enclosed my resumé setting forth additional information on my background and experience. I will contact you by telephone on September 21 to discuss this situation further.

Best regards,

Frank Beenaneagle

Frank's introduction letter effectively sells his transition from lawyer to business development executive:

- He lets Joan know immediately the type of job he is seeking.
- Frank showcases and translates his international legal experience into business expertise by referencing his Central and South American work, in particular, his handling of the Argentina project. Notice how he orients John by giving specific information about each project.
- Frank shows his knowledge of Leading's business by mentioning their recent Mexico contract. He uses that development to create a need for further development activities. He, of course, offers to fill that need.
- He shows interest by informing Joan when he will contact her.

These sample letters provide a framework for you to develop your own introduction letter fitting your particular style and qualifications. To reiterate, the keys to writing successful introduction letters are:

- research
- specificity with regard to the job sought after
- translating legal talents to specific business needs
- energy
- professionalism

> *The best way to make your dreams*
> *come true is to wake up.*
> -Paul Valery
> (early-twentieth-century French poet)

Tailoring Your Resumé

Your resumé should accompany your introduction letter. The introduction letter interests the prospective employers enough so that they want to know more about you. Your resumé is available to provide them with more information. Your resumé extends your introduction letter. What this means is the resumé, first and foremost, must not detract from the introduction letter. The resumé must complement the introduction letter.

Reaffirm and support what you said in your introduction letter in your resumé. Have nothing in the resumé that does not support the introduction letter. This means that since you are writing a targeted introduction letter; you must write a targeted resumé as well. Let us look at some ways to do this with your resumé.

Form

A Word About Length

Discard right away the popular notion that resumés must be one page long. There is no magical, legal, or optimal length for resumés. If five pages supports your introduction letter, then use five pages. I realize this flies in the face of the popular how-to-write-resumé books. I do not know how this idea got started, but it just does not make any sense. What should a resumé do? The resumé should complement your introduction letter by informing and selling the prospective employer. You are *informing* and *selling*. Why confine your resumé to just one page? If you need more space to inform and sell the reader, then use the space you need to do so. It is like paying for thirty seconds of advertising air time and only using ten seconds of it. A note of explanation is in order. The example resumés that follow are all about one page long. These resumés are set out to give you an idea of style, technique, and content within the confines of limited space here. Do not restrict yourself in this manner. However, if one page is all you need, that is fine. Just do not limit yourself.

The vast majority of resumés look the same. Why? They look the same because the vast majority of job seekers do not put enough of their own thought or effort into writing them. They use a form resumé out of a book as a template. Then, all that is left to do is slap together one page of seemingly unrelated data that ends up reading like an obituary notice, make a lot of copies of it, and mail it out to as many places as they have postage. Of course, they whine because no one calls them for an interview! Approach this differently. You already have, or are about to, write a dynamic, guided introduction letter. It is pointless to draft a winning introduction letter if you are going to attach a mass-produced obit notice to it. Decide now to put in the work required. Before you get underway writing a better resumé suited to your particular qualifications and the job you are after, look at the following.

What Not to Do

I may surprise you because many of these what-not-to-do's appear on most of the mass-produced resumés. So, how can they be wrong if so many people do them? I compiled the following list from input from people who read lots of resumés. These things annoy them. Remember, in order to favorably impress someone, you want to put yourself in their shoes and see yourself as they see you. It is hard to impress someone whom you have just annoyed.

So, please *do not:*

- Label parts of the resumé, such as Work Experience, Education, Career Objective. The readers are smart enough to know what these entries are without you telling them.
- Mention your undergraduate GPA. That is past history and no longer relevant.
- List non-job related personal facts, like marital status, kids' names, height, weight, and condition of your health. Again, all that is irrelevant. Or, at least it should be.
- Expound on, or even mention, your hobbies, unless they *directly relate* to the job you are after. Although it may be fascinating to you, not many people will care about your stamp collection. You will see how to handle this area later on.

One thing that really bugs me when I pick up a resumé is to see RESUMÉ written on the top. Like the applicant thinks I've never seen one of these before! It gets me off on the wrong foot with the writer. I know it's a little thing, but it really irritates me.

And then, there is RECOMMENDATIONS AVAILABLE UPON REQUEST. We all know that. It's almost as if they think you will not believe what they are saying, so you can ask someone else.
-Human relations manager for a Fortune 500 company

Hopefully, you will avoid these long-standing irritants. We are still not through with looking at the form. As with any advertisement, format sells. Let us look at resumé format.

Selecting a Format

In the world of resumés, there are two basic types of formats. There is the *topical* format resumé and the *chronological* format resumé. A topical format resumé highlights skills that you believe you have and the job you are after requires. This resumé format stresses skills and infers experience. A chronological format resumé focuses on jobs you have had, when you had them, and what you did at them. This resumé format stresses work experience and infers skills. So that you can see the difference, the following set of resumés show how the same applicant's qualifications, education, and work experience might appear in the two types of resumés. Do not study the resumés for the purpose of learning how to write your own. Just notice how each one presents the information.

First, we examine the topical format resumé.

JANET SMITH

1400 Jackson Street
Midway City, PA 15200
(412) 765-4321

I want to utilize my communications and marketing skills, in combination with my knowledge of computer systems and software, as a Marketing Director for a business computer systems company.

COMMUNICATIONS AND MARKETING:
As Marketing Manager for *Small Business Enterprise* Magazine, a national publication devoted to operating and enhancing the small business, I oversaw all aspects of marketing. Over a three year period, I increased circulation by over 25% through an aggressive direct mail campaign and trade show advertising throughout the United States. I worked with small business owners, including computer systems companies, and venture capitalists to determine what issues they wanted addressed in a publication such as ours. I also showed them how they could benefit from our magazine, both as a subscriber and as an advertiser.

I conducted seminars for small business owners on various aspects of their business operations. These seminars benefited the small business owners and effectively marketed my employer to target customers. Several new clients were added as a result of these seminars.

Member of the American Marketing Association.

COMPUTER HARDWARE AND SOFTWARE:
I sold personal computers to individuals and small business owners. I recommended hardware systems and software that met the needs and budgets of the customer. In order to do this, I developed an extensive knowledge of personal computer models and kept myself current with the new developments in them by attending trade show seminars and reading literature provided by the various computer manufacturers.

I also have firsthand knowledge of how computers operate through repairing and servicing central processing units and associated peripherals as a member of the service department.

Member of the Midway City Computer Club

1987   BA English, Midway University

Here is Janet's employment and education data set out in a
chronological format resumé.

JANET SMITH   1400 JACKSON STREET
                                         MIDWAY CITY, PA 15200
                                         (412) 765-4321

I want to utilize my communications and marketing skills, in combination with
my knowledge of computer systems and software, as a Marketing Director for a
business computer systems company.

January 1993 to Present
Marketing Manager, *Small Business Enterprise* Magazine
          Philadelphia, PA

I designed and implemented marketing activities, including a direct mail campaign and trade show advertising that resulted in a 25% increase in circulation
over a three year period. I expanded the reader/customer base of small business owners, business suppliers, including computer suppliers, and venture capitalists as both subscribers and advertisers.

January 1989 to January 1993
Account Representative, Forbes & Forbes Business Consultants
          Philadelphia, PA

I implemented strategies for small business owners to enhance their profitability. I
conducted seminars on various aspects of their business and as a way of name
recognition for the firm with a target group of customers. Several new clients
were obtained through this method of advertising.

December 1988 to January 1989
Sales Associate, Computer World
          Philadelphia, PA

I sold personal computers to individuals and small business owners after evaluating their needs and budgets. I developed job-related knowledge of all major
suppliers' personal computer lines and emerging technology. I did this by
attending trade show seminars and by reading computer suppliers' information
literature.

January 1988 to December 1988
Service Technician, Computer World

Upon completing the in-house computer service course, I repaired and serviced
personal computers and peripherals in the service department.

1987   BA English Midway University

Midway Computer Club; American Marketing Association

Still Yet Another One to Overcome

Let us examine another resumé writing truism. That is, that job seekers with limited work experience, such as recent graduates, should use a topical format resumé because it showcases their skills and hides their limited experience. Does it really? Look at Janet's topical format resumé. Are you sure when she acquired these skills? In what context did she acquire them? The problem with the topical resumé is that it hides the applicant's experience a little too much. The reader cannot really figure out where the applicant learned these skills. This is not good. Because when the reader cannot figure something out about you, he or she will just move on to the next applicant. Why should an employer waste time figuring out your situation? There are dozens of applicants waiting in the wings.

Why not try to get the best of both worlds? Merge the two resumé format styles and create a *merged format* resumé. The merged format resumé highlights the applicant's skills and informs the reader when, where, and how these skills were acquired. Hiding perceived deficiencies is never a good idea. Raise the issues and deal with them on your terms. Dealing with problems on your terms gives you the best chance to put an employer at ease. Observe how Janet looks with a merged format resumé.

JANET SMITH

1400 Jackson Street
Midway City, PA
(412) 765-4321

I want to utilize my communications and marketing skills, in combination with my knowledge of computer systems and software, as a Marketing Director for a business computer systems company

COMMUNICATIONS AND MARKETING
As marketing manager for a magazine devoted to small business, I designed and implemented a marketing program that resulted in a 25% increase in circulation over a three year period. I developed a rapport with reader/customer base of small business owners, business suppliers, including computer suppliers, and venture capitalists. Through these discussions, I determined the topics and issues they wanted to read and be informed about. By tailoring the magazine to their needs, they saw value for themselves as subscribers and advertisers.

As an account representative for a business consultant, I implemented strategies for small business clients to enhance their profitability. I conducted seminars on various aspects of their business and as a way of name recognition for the firm. By targeting our marketing effort in this manner, the firm was able to add several new clients for very few advertising dollars.

COMPUTER HARDWARE AND SOFTWARE
As a computer sales associate for a computer store, I sold personal computers to the general public and small business owners after helping them evaluate their needs. I handled all major suppliers of personal computers.

As a technician trained through the formal in-house program, I repaired personal computers and peripherals in the service department.

January 1993 to Present
Marketing Manager, Small Business Enterprise Magazine
            Philadelphia, PA

January 1989 to January 1993
Account Representative, Forbes & Forbes Business Consultants
            Philadelphia, PA

December 1988 to January 1989
Sales Associate, Computer World
            Philadelphia, PA

January 1988 to December 1988
Service Technician, Computer World
            Philadelphia, PA

1987   BA English Midway University

Member, Midway Computer Club; Member, American Marketing Association

Notice how Janet sets out the skills she believes are important for the job and that she feels she has. In addition, you can see her work experience from where she acquired these skills. Actually, Janet has some pretty good experience, so a chronological format resumé would serve her better. However, as I stated earlier, the purpose of looking at these resumés is to see their form and how each one presents the information. The chronological format resumé and the merged format resumé have their own distinct advantages. However, it probably makes the most sense to utilize the merged format resumé if you are a recent law school graduate with little work experience. Conversely, if you are a practicing attorney with a lot of relevant experience, you will want to stay with the chronological format resumé.

My son recently graduated from college and was looking for a job. I asked him for his resumé so that I could give it to some of my contacts. You know, kind of help the kid out. Well, I took one look at his resumé and realized he didn't know anything more about how to get a job than all of the other applicants whose resumés I had read. My son has a lot of good skills and is a good worker. Although, I'll admit, you'd never be able to figure that out from his resumé. I guess I thought because he was my son, he'd have some inherited knowledge.

-Partner in an executive search firm

You are now ready to use our earlier applicants, with their varying experience levels, to see how you might create your resumé to complement your introduction letter. I will begin with Ellen. Ellen was the recent graduate seeking a public relations job. She has little work experience. However, as with all law school graduates, her skills are strong. First, review Ellen's introduction letter on the next page. Then, examine the following sample resumé, which Ellen could use to accompany her introduction letter.

ELLEN LEGALEAGLE
123 Main Street
Law City, NY 11202
(212) 765-4321

September 1, 1997

Ms. Mary Employer
Director of Public Relations
Leading Edge Company
1 World Plaza
Business City, NY 11000

Dear Ms. Employer:

May I help you as an associate public relations specialist?

I want to put my communications skills to work. I have recently completed law school course work designed to further develop my skills for a career in business. I participated in mock trial and moot court competitions throughout my entire law school career. In so doing, I have experienced representing a client to the public, both in the printed and spoken media, under the most adverse circumstances. My training included having experienced attorneys and actors coach me on improving my presentations and rapport with juries, clients, and audiences. Developing rapport is the essence of lawyering, and I want to bring this into my public relations career.

My formalized training includes business related courses giving me a solid foundation in contracts, agency and partnership, labor law, intellectual property, business organization, and employment law. I can relate to the issues that Leading Edge Company encounters conducting business because I have studied business from the issues confrontation perspective. This background understanding lets me think on my feet a little easier than most people in the field.

I want to be part of a ground-breaking software company. Your recent development of the XYZ software is quite exciting and puts Leading Edge ahead of its closest competitors, Alpha Corporation and Beta Company. The next step of informing and selling the public will be critical to your success. I can assist you in this important area.

I have enclosed my résumé providing additional information. I will contact you, by telephone, on September 21 to discuss your interest.

Best regards,

Ellen Legaleagle

ELLEN LEGALEAGLE

123 Main Street
Law City, NY 11202
(212) 765-4321

I am seeking an entry level public relations specialist position with a rapidly evolving company in the technology sector. I want to utilize my marketing and business skills developed from past job experience and law school course work.

COMMUNICATIONS AND MARKETING
As an account manager, I developed direct ad campaigns for expanding businesses, many of which were computer companies.

- developed a direct ad campaign with their technicians and marketing staff to target customers
- created ads in magazines and other media showcasing the strengths of the various client companies
- conducted surveys to determine consumer demand for certain products and services. These surveys spanned the spectrum from one-on-one meetings with representatives of large buyers to using industry group databases
- test marketed various products and services

I participated in mock trial competitions throughout my law school career where I had to represent various clients under adversarial circumstances, both in civil and criminal proceedings. The civil proceedings included situations involving deceptive trade practices and industrial pollution. The criminal action stemmed from violations of federal environmental statutes. Related to this work, my environmental law course work included drafting and issuing press releases discussing various incidents of pollution and then following up with representatives of citizen and regulatory groups.

BUSINESS SKILLS
As an account manager, I developed business plans for various clients as part of the service we provided as part of securing client accounts. I formulated the business plans after visiting with the client and with its customers. I incorporated where they wanted to take the company with their present financial situation and where their respective customer bases appeared to be headed.

My law school course work includes business-related course work in contracts, agency and partnership, labor law, intellectual property, business organizations, and employment law.

September 1991 to August 1993
Assistant Account Manager, XYZ Advertising Company
Minneapolis, MN

1996   JD American Law School
1991   BA English University of Minnesota

Member, Law City Computer Club; Member, Public Relations Society of America

Ellen, like most recently graduated law students, does not have a lot of work experience. The merged format resumé is appropriate for her. She states early on in the objective that she has marketing and business skills developed from both work experience and law school course work. She goes on to prove this in the body of her resumé. Notice how the resumé discussed what she did in her job and did not just list some vague duties. She discusses the specifics of the direct ad campaign, conducting customer surveys, and developing business plans. All of these activities are of interest to Mary Employer because they develop skills applicable to the public relations field.

The resumé also brings in her course work to complement her introduction letter. She does more than merely list law school courses. She relates them to the public relations field by, for instance, talking about drafting and issuing press releases discussing pollution incidents.

Ellen mentions her membership in the Law City Computer Club and the Public Relations Society of America because belonging to these particular groups shows her interest in relevant areas of the job she is seeking. She omits other hobbies and interests that are not job related.

You can observe a lot just by watching.
-Yogi Berra
(philosopher and professional baseball player)

Job seekers should look upon their cover letter and resumé as their portfolio. Kind of like a model or an artist. It is what they've actually done. Models do not just tell you in a resumé that they look good; they show you some photos. Artists do not apply for jobs just by telling you they can draw or paint; they have a portfolio of their work. Same thing should be for anyone looking for a job. Show me what you've done somewhere, whether it's in school or in your previous job, even if that job was waiting tables.

-President of an international food packaging company

Now, observe how John, a practicing attorney wanting to enter the business sector, might set up his resumé to accompany his introduction letter. John practiced in the employment law area. Review his introduction letter on the next page before looking at his resumé.

JOHN LEGALEAGLE

123 Main Street
Law City, NY 11202
(212) 765-4321

September 1, 1997

Mr. John Employer
Leading Energy Corporation
2 World Plaza
Business City, NY 11000

Dear Mr. Employer:

Are you in need of a human resources specialist able to deal with the difficult problems facing companies as employers?

Practicing law for ten years has exposed me to a variety of labor and employment issues, including job discrimination and sexual harassment claims. Now I would like to put my experience to work for you. I can recognize and deal with these problem situations early on before they become adversarial. Early action prevents yesterday's predictable situations from becoming today's problems and tomorrow's lawsuits and unfavorable publicity. The most looming example of such a problem situation is the issue of wrongful firing. Primary Energy Corporation is being sued in this area by a former employee. My sources tell me that they will not be alone in this arena. I can head off problems such as these because I have been on the other side and know how to prevent these unfortunate situations from occurring. I spent two years of private practice interviewing former employees and their employers and subsequently developing strategies to represent former employees. The vast majority of the cases followed similar patterns yielding predictable consequences.

I want to work for a company that is creating its own future such as Leading Energy is. Your energy swap transactions have made you a leader in the energy business. As your work becomes more complex, your employee needs will follow suit. Unfortunately, so do some problems. If you want to be ready for the future in the human resources area, in the same way as you are in the energy area, I would like to talk with you.

I have enclosed my resumé providing additional information on my training and experience. I will follow up by phone on September 21 and see if there is a mutual interest.

Sincerely,

John Legaleagle

JOHN LEGALEAGLE

123 Main Street
Law City, NY 11202
(212) 765-4321

I am seeking a personnel specialist position within a fast moving company where creative problem solving and highly developed interpersonal skills add value. I have dealt with difficult employment issues and am looking for the opportunity to apply my years of experience. I want to develop and implement strategies to help the company address upcoming employment issues.

January 1985 to Present
Staff Attorney, Parker, Jones, and Adams
        Law City, NY

As a staff attorney, I represented Fortune 500 companies, including companies in the energy sector, involved in hiring discrimination and sexual harassment litigation. By being in all parts of the litigation process of several of these cases, I have firsthand knowledge of how these unfortunate situations arise.

    I interviewed plaintiffs, defendants and witnesses. Discussions with them were quite telling and these situations all develop along similar patterns.

    From these years of work, I have developed hiring and termination guidelines for several companies. I designed these guidelines to avoid the situations leading up to the problems that become subjects of litigation in the employment and labor area.

    These companies have reported a significant reduction of employee related problems in the wrongful firing and harassment areas.

September 1983 to January 1985
Winston and Churchill
Law City, NY

I represented clients in harassment and discrimination litigation against former employers. I became familiar with these problems by interviewing all of the parties and analyzing the situations. The outcome is predictable when certain situations arise. Avoid problems by recognizing these situations and addressing them sooner, rather than later.

1983   JD American Law School
1979   BS Biology University of Vermont

American Bar Association—Energy Law Section

Since John has some good work experience, he has chosen the chronological format resume. Notice how he establishes that he has relevant business experience in the objective. He explains what it is, in detail, and how he came to attain it. John mentions specific employment issues that he worked on. He showed how what he learned can be valuable to a prospective employer. He emphasizes what he can do right now by citing the guidelines he wrote for previous clients. Because of the specificity the reader knows that John can easily translate his legal skills to personnel specialist skills. When you just mention vague skills without supplying specifics, you will not accomplish this.

John mentions that he is a member of the Energy Law Section of the American Bar Association. This links him to the energy industry. Also, by being a member of this section, he can develop valuable contacts in this fast growing business sector.

Out of every fruition of success,
no matter what, comes forth something
to make a new effort necessary.
-Walt Whitman
(nineteenth-century American poet)

Let us return to another example of a recent graduate with minimal work experience. Karen Neweagle is seeking a job as a marketer in the packaging sector. Her introduction letter discussed earlier, sets out her presentation.

KAREN NEWEAGLE
123 Main Street
Law City, NY 11202
(212) 765-4321

September 1, 1997

Ms. Mary Employer
Vice President of Marketing
Leading Packaging Corporation
3 World Plaza
Business City, NY 11000

Dear Ms. Employer:

May I be of help to you in an entry level capacity in marketing Leading Packaging's new line of frozen food packaging?

Selling; whether it is a position or a product, is the essence of my training and experience. I recently graduated from law school where I won several mock trial advocacy awards. I was also quite successful on my college debate team. In both activities, I have benefited from the coaching of practicing attorneys and actors to learn how to effectively make a point. I have spent a lot of hours and worked hard to make it look easy. Now, I want to use my skills to help your marketing effort. I want to be out in front where all the action is.

I am familiar with introducing new product lines. I was a sales associate in an upscale clothing store. New product lines are synonymous with the fashion industry. I learned first hand how new lines are tested and then brought in. This is where I developed my interest in marketing new product lines.

I realize the goal of marketers is to get the customer to sign a contract. My law school course work included intensive course work in contracts. I have an added advantage in that I have seen what makes good contracts, as well as bad ones. I have learned from the expertise and misfortune of others. My training has also given me a solid grounding in the structuring of business organizations, such as partnerships, joint ventures and corporations. Leading Packaging routinely deals with all of these business structures.

I want to take my energy and skills to a company that displays similar high energy and innovation. Leading Packaging is certainly at the top of the list as it posts the highest return on assets of all the packaging firms. The new frozen food packaging line will help Leading Packaging stay ahead of your competitors. I can help that happen.

I have enclosed my resumé providing additional information on my background and training. I will follow up by telephone on September 21 that we may talk further.

Best regards,

Karen Neweagle

Here's Karen's resumé:

KAREN NEWEAGLE

123 Main Street
Law City, NY 11202
(212) 765-4321

I am interested in an entry level account manager position for a fast moving, innovative company. Introducing new product lines interests me and I want to utilize my business and marketing skills in this area.

MARKETING
As a sales associate at an upscale clothing store in the Dallas area, I was involved in the marketing of new clothing lines for women. I experienced firsthand the importance of understanding all of the important aspects of your target market such as tastes and budget. The store was in a constant state of introducing new clothing lines and styles. The fact that some succeeded, and others did not, interested me.

I want to utilize that experience and translate it into other types of selling. One of the criteria for the successful introduction of clothing lines was to communicate information about the new lines in ways that appealed to the target audience. This appeared to be one of the most decisive indicators of success. Marketing is communication with your customers. To that end, my law school experience was invaluable.

I won several mock trial advocacy awards. I was also quite successful on my college debate team. Years of speaking in public have made me relaxed in this type of activity. This type of face-to-face communicating I gives me the skills to introduce and sell new products.

BUSINESS
As a sales associate, I became familiar with the daily operations of a clothing store. This day-to-day familiarity served as a good reference for my law school course work that was business oriented.

My law school course work included intensive course work in contracts. My training on how business organizations, such as partnerships, joint ventures and corporations are structured has been quite useful in helping me understand why certain transactions occur.

January 1991 to December 1993
Assistant Manager, Stylish Woman Clothing Store
                    Dallas, Texas

1996   JD American Law University
1991   BA Fine Arts The University of Texas

   American Marketing Association

Karen blended her limited work experience and her law school course work to create a solid background to land a marketing job. Notice that her research informed her of the new product line that she was able to relate to her experience at the clothing store. This gives her a decided advantage over other applicants who used mass produced, generic resumés. Her resumé sells her skills and experience. She tells Mary about what she did in law school so that Mary can relate to Karen's experience. The resumé proactively sells; it does not read like an obituary. Lastly, she mentioned her membership in the American Marketing Association to indicate her interest in this part of the business. This is just another way she shows that she has stepped from the legal world to the business world.

Your Resumé Must Relate You to the Reader

I can't say that I recommend that every applicant do this, but one applicant sent me a photocopy of her company's annual report that had a couple of paragraphs on a particular project the company had successfully completed. She circled the writing on the page and wrote: I WAS THE PROJECT LEADER. We called her in for an interview the next day. She didn't have a resumé. She just sent that photocopy and her phone number.

-Human resources director of a
computer manufacturing company

Only a mediocre person is at his very best all the time.
-William Somerset Maugham
(early-twentieth-century English playwright and novelist)

Next is William, another recent law school graduate. He is seeking a position as an assistant corporate trainer in a manufacturing company that has recently expanded its operations. Review his introduction letter on the next page.

WILLIAM LEGALEAGLE
123 MAIN STREET
LAW CITY, NY 11202
(212) 765-4321

September 1, 1997

Ms. Samantha Employer
Head Corporate Trainer
Universal Manufacturing Corporation
3 World Plaza
Business City, NY 11000

Dear Ms. Employer:

Are you in need of an assistant corporate trainer in light of Universal's recent expansion into the communications equipment manufacturing sector?

I want to put the communications and teaching skills I have developed in law school to work as a corporate trainer. I have recently completed my law school course work in which I concentrated on communicating difficult, and sometimes controversial, ideas to groups of people. Mock trial and moot court participation and various clinic courses in trial advocacy, client counseling, and negotiations seminars have given me the benefit of the experience of practicing attorneys to improve my presentations. This intense training regime developed my communication and organization skills needed to effectively train employees in new skills.

My training also emphasized research and writing skills designed to effectively discuss and persuade through clear and concise writing. My writing project was a fifty-page paper requiring hours of research, and many further hours, to distill the information into informative and persuasive writing. Most of this research was computer-assisted so I have a working knowledge of computers I can demonstrate to others.

Universal has timed its expansion well to take advantage of the exploding growth in the communications sector. In order to capitalize on this expansion, your group will have to train and motivate the work force. I would like to help with that endeavor and believe I can assist your group.

I have enclosed my resumé setting out additional information regarding my background and training. I will contact you, by telephone, on September 21 to discuss this further.

Best regards,

William Legaleagle

Now, read William's resumé.

WILLIAM LEGALEAGLE

123 Main Street
Law City, NY 11000
(212) 765-4321

I want to put the communications and teaching skills I have developed in law school to work as an associate corporate trainer. I want to contribute not only by teaching, but through utilizing my research and writing skills to help develop the programs needed to keep your employees productive.

COMMUNICATIONS AND TEACHING SKILLS
My law school training heavily emphasized communicating and explaining a position or point of view. I participated throughout my law school career in trial advocacy clinics, seminars, and competitions. I had the benefit of skilled practitioners to coach and critique my presentations. As I became more accomplished, I began teaching the less experienced students how to improve their presentations. It was in doing this that I became aware of how much I enjoyed teaching others and wanted to continue doing it as a career.

RESEARCH AND WRITING SKILLS
As a complement to the course work emphasizing oral communication, I also had continuous exposure to research and writing. I had three semesters of legal research and writing. Experienced writers reviewed and critiqued my work. This course work laid the foundation for extracurricular competitions involving research and writing. This all culminated with my 50-page research paper needed for graduation.

January 1995 to December 1995
Teaching Assistant; First Year Trial Advocacy Program

1996   JD American Law School
1992   BA History University of Florida

Notice that William does not have any work experience. This is not that unusual. Many students go right into law school after graduating from college. All William can talk to an employer about is the skills and experience he gained from law school. William does a very good job with what he has. He knows the skills required to be an effective corporate trainer from his research into the job. He specifically mentions how he has these skills and how he came about acquiring them.

Again, notice how William's research told him about Universal's plans to expand. Samantha should realize that although William has no business experience, he is actively trying to involve himself in it. These kinds of things really make a difference with prospective employers.

> *I am only an average man, but I work*
> *harder at it than the average man.*
> -Theodore Roosevelt

Katherine is our next applicant. She has two years of work experience as legal counsel. She now wants to move into the business consulting field. Because she has strong experience, Katherine will use the chronological format resumé. First, review her introduction letter.

KATHERINE LEGALEAGLE
123 Main Street
Law City, NY 11000
(212) 765-4321

September 1, 1997

Mr. Robert Employer
Stamford Business Consultants
6 World Plaza
Business City, NY 11000

Dear Mr. Employer:

I want to apply my business skills and experience as an account executive for a consulting firm having a client base of fast moving, innovative companies.

I have been an associate corporate counsel for a medium size specialty steel products manufacturing firm for the past two years. I have been part of the negotiating teams involved with sales contracts of specialty pressurized steel containers both to domestic and international customers. The total value of these sales contracts was on the order of $10 million. On the other side, I have negotiated supply contracts with vendors for raw materials for feedstock in the steel-making process and for natural gas as fuel for the manufacturing plant. In so doing, I have become familiar with the manufacturing operations and financials. My interests, as a result of participating in these projects, have shifted into a broader business range. I believe my manufacturing experience will make me an asset to your consulting group.

Your consulting firm interests me because of your work with specialty mills, in particular with those that are exporting their products. I understand that your team helped American Specialty Steel Company land a large order with an Australian-based petroleum refiner in the process of expanding. My international experience includes working with Asian and southeastern European customers. I was on a project team responsible for a $5 million sale of specialty steel goods to Pakistan. Prior to that, I was on the team working on a turnkey arrangement to fabricate a specialty mini-mill in Thailand. I want to make the change into the consulting area where I can use my experience and add upon it.

I have enclosed my resumé setting forth additional information on my background and experience. I will contact you by telephone on September 21 to discuss any mutual interest.

Best regards,

Katherine Legaleagle

Katherine's chronological format resumé expands upon her introduction letter.

KATHERINE LEGALEAGLE

123 Main Street
Law City, NY 11000
(212) 765-4321

I want to apply my business skills and experience as a management consultant associate to work with a consulting firm with a client base of fast moving, innovative companies.

May 1995 to Present
Associate Corporate Counsel, Specialty Steel Products, Inc.
Industrytown, NY 11001

Specialty Steel is one of the largest suppliers of pressurized steel vessels in the world. As associate counsel, I was part of several negotiating teams involved with sales contracts with domestic and foreign buyers needing pressurized containers for their manufacturing processes. I not only had to understand how our process system operated but I also became familiar with the manufacturing processes of refiners, other steel makers, and auto makers. I spent several weeks on different occasions in the facilities of customers to understand their needs with regard to pressurized vessels.

I negotiated contracts with natural gas suppliers for Specialty's fuel supply. We were able to lower our fuel costs by over 10% from the previous year. Similarly, I negotiated long-term contracts with ore suppliers. By fixing the cost of ore for a five year period, Specialty was able to aggressively bid on several foreign projects that were very price competitive.

I have overseas experience with Australian, Asian, and European firms. My experience involved upgrading existing refineries and manufacturing plants in the host country. Success in selling required plant visits and a working knowledge of each customer's operations.

I have attended several seminars on negotiating with foreign customers in order to better prepare myself for this type of work.

1995   JD American Law University
1991   BS Chemistry University of Pennsylvania

Member, Specialty Steel Makers of America

Katherine has some very good experience as an attorney that she translates into the business sector. Her success at doing this confirms that the chronological format resumé is the preferred way to highlight her talents. Notice how she states some different specifics from her introduction letter and gives quite a bit of detail about the specialty steel business and her work with overseas customers. This shows the employer that she is savvy in the business arena and will be able to contribute immediately. Her resumé closely follows the introduction letter; complementing it and expanding upon it.

There are risks and costs to a program of action.
But they are far less than the long-range risks
and costs of comfortable inaction.
-John F. Kennedy

I believe one of the biggest mistakes that job applicants make is that they try to summarize their lives in too short of a document. If they want to have a short document, they would be much better off explaining, in detail, their biggest accomplishment. With over 95% of the resumés and cover letters that I have had to read, the writer never tells you specifically what he or she has accomplished. It is very tough to give someone a job based on general statements about what a good person they are, or how they are a hard worker.
-Vice president of Fortune 500 energy firm

Mark is our next applicant. Recall that Mark is a recent graduate with no work experience. He wants to enter into the education and training sector. Mark will have to relate his law school experience to working in this sector in order to show a prospective employer that he can add value.

MARK LEGALEAGLE
123 MAIN STREET
LAW CITY, NY 11202
(212) 765-4321

September 1, 1997

Ms. Susan Employer
President
NewMethod Educational Systems
8 World Plaza
Business City, NY 11000

Dear Ms. Employer:

I want to be part of your company's growth by designing and marketing packaged educational materials.

My undergraduate and law school coursework required successfully communicating my ideas. Legal training stresses the importance of precise and persuasive written and oral communication. Being a part of your company's efforts to develop innovative educational courses is exciting. I enjoy designing creative ways to teach and communicate with others.

In law school, I observed that some students found group study effective—others found that they needed to develop their own learning programs. Just as an attorney needs to target his arguments to persuade the jury, so one needs to tailor one's teaching methods to the student. Your individualized packaged reading and math programs are an excellent example of doing just that.

Because law school requires a lot of writing, faculty experienced and trained in effective communication train us to be effective writers. I want to use this training and experience to help others improve their writing skills. I feel I can contribute to your company's work in this area.

I have enclosed my resumé setting forth additional information on my training and background. I will contact you, by telephone, on September 21 to see if we might discuss my ideas further.

Best regards,

Mark Legaleagle

Mark uses a merged format type of resumé because he has no work experience.

MARK LEGALEAGLE

123 Main Street
Law City, NY 11202
(212) 765-4321

I want to be part of an entrepreneurial company's growth by designing and marketing packaged educational materials. My law school work provided me experience in communicating ideas and methods. How to teach these ideas and methods effectively interests me.

COMMUNICATIONS
I have had three writing courses and seminars taught by faculty members or practicing lawyers dedicated to improving my writing skills. I wrote on various legal issues. Writing professionals then critiqued my work. It was in these classes that I developed my interest and ideas on how to improve anyone's ability to write better.

I had similar course work regarding speaking skills. I presented various topics and issues to the class. Professional speakers and actors then critiqued my presentations so as to improve them. Many of the same ideas and concepts involved with writing were present here.

LEARNING AND TEACHING
Law school training requires that you learn to teach yourself because no lawyer can know all of the current laws. I believe learning quickly and effectively is the key to being a good attorney. I found that not only did I learn to educate myself, but I taught some of my classmates as well. By explaining concepts to others, you learn them better yourself and you are able to communicate them more clearly. The traditional lecture methods of teaching were not always effective. One can see this more clearly when one is a student and a teacher at the same time.

1996   JD American Law School
1993   BA English Literature University of Maryland

Mark's resumé complements his introduction letter. Because he has no work experience, he only has his course work to discuss. He does a good job with what he has. He relates his course work to the two skills that interest the employer—communicating and teaching. This introduction letter and resumé should be able to land an interview with Susan.

Let us look at one last applicant. Frank is a practicing attorney with some good experience as a member of several negotiating teams for his current employer. So, he will want to use a chronological format resumé and emphasize his experience as a lawyer in business experience terms. First, review is his introduction letter.

FRANK BEENANEAGLE
123 Main Street
Law City, NY 11202
(212) 765-4321

September 1, 1997

Ms. Joan Employer
Vice President of Marketing
Leading Import-Export Company
4 World Plaza
Business City, NY 11000

Dear Ms. Employer:

Do you need a business development professional with several years of international experience?

I have practiced law in the international arena for the past five years. I have negotiated and drafted partnership and joint venture agreements with industry partners from Central America and South America. I am particularly proud of a $30 million joint venture project in Argentina that I helped get back on track after the parties had closed off their discussions. This sense of accomplishment resulting from successful facilitating and negotiating is now what I am seeking. Business development is where I want to focus my interest and expertise.

I want to work for Leading because of its commitment to developing the Central American and South American markets. Your recent contract to supply oilfield equipment to Pemex leaves you well positioned for further work in Mexico and Central America. I can help develop those markets for you. I am fluent in both spoken and written Spanish. I have worked with Pemex on several occasions. Most recently I worked on a $10 million sales contract involving specially fabricated oilfield production equipment. This contract was one of the first such arrangements consummated in Mexico. I would like to give Leading the benefit of my experience and expertise.

I have enclosed my resumé setting forth additional information on my background and experience. I will contact you by telephone on September 21 to discuss this situation further.

Best regards,

Frank Beenaneagle

Notice how his resumé nicely complements and expands upon his introduction letter.

FRANK BEENANEAGLE   123 Main Street
                                          Law City, NY 11202
                                          (212) 765-4321

I am seeking a position as business development manager in the international area. I prefer an area of responsibility in South America or Central America so that I can utilize my contacts and experience and Spanish fluency.

July 1991 to Present
Senior Staff Attorney, Worldwide Engineering
                    Houston, Texas

I negotiated and drafted partnership agreements for joint venture pipeline projects and turnkey construction projects in Mexico, Argentina, Panama, Brazil, and Puerto Rico. These ventures helped make Worldwide Engineering one of the ten most active engineering firms in the world on a project basis as measured in amount of capital invested.

As part of my preparation for these various projects, I completed in-house sponsored Spanish classes. I am fluent, both orally and written, in Spanish. As a result of this language fluency, I am comfortable in Central and South American cities and have developed friendships with many of my foreign customers.

Last year, I participated in a project development team involved on a refinery expansion project for PEMEX in Mexico City. The project was to help PEMEX increase its refining capacity by 50% in one of its largest plants. I negotiated directly with PEMEX representatives and worked to help both parties achieve their objectives. This project closed shortly thereafter and construction is now underway. My work on this project led to my interest in international business development.

In addition to the above, I was instrumental in bringing a pipeline joint venture to conclusion in Brazil. The project involved a 200-mile petroleum products pipeline from the Brazilian refining area to the outskirts of a major urban area. The project finished on time and within budget. This project helped launch my firm into the international arena and led to the Mexico City refinery project.

1988   JD American Law School
1983   BS Political Science University of Florida

American Bar Association—International Division

Frank did a good job of translating his experience as an attorney into business experience. He convincingly showed that he is ready for the business sector and that he is ready to leave the legal one. Joan should have no trouble being convinced that Frank can handle a business development position. Again, I recommend the chronological format because Frank has excellent experience that he can showcase.

> *Do what you can,*
> *with what you have,*
> *where you are.*
> -Theodore Roosevelt

Writing Your Introduction Letter and Resumé

Now it is up to you to create your own introduction letter and resumé. To sum up, the following will help you create the winning finished product to get you an interview for the career you want:

- Research potential target companies. This will set up a nexus for your skills and experience and what the company needs in the person who will fill the position.
- Be specific. Specifics help the reader infer skills. Readers ignore vague generalities.
- You want a job in the business sector. Relate you law school experience and work experience in business terms, specifically in the terms that interest the target employer.

Once you have satisfactorily completed these documents, you are ready to mail them to the *triple points*. Remember, you must mail these important documents to a person. Make sure it is a person in charge of the hiring process.

I provide these to guide you in obtaining the relevant and specific information about the target company and about you. Again, if you choose to use your own system, that's fine; just make sure you have collected and are presenting specific and relevant information.

I read a lot of resumés where it looks like the applicant has some real good experience. But he or she is usually so vague or only writes a sentence or two about it, that you really do not know what they did. And when you're not sure, you just go on to the next applicant.

-Vice president of marketing for
a business consulting firm

Do Not Just Sit There Waiting

You say you will follow up by phone on a prearranged certain date. Do it. You more than double your chances of getting an interview when you follow up your correspondence with a phone call. However, just do not call and hope something comes into your head. The follow-up call is another opportunity to sell yourself. Have an outline of the key sales points you want to make before the call. Start by prepping yourself. Keep the introduction letter and resumé in front of you so that you know what you wrote. Again, do not finesse this. You are looking for an interview.

How hard somebody works to get a job is a good indication of how hard that person will work on the job. One-size-fits-all resumés and cover letters say LAZY PERSON to me. I do not want that kind of person in my organization.

-Computer company entrepreneur

Research you have done will help lay the groundwork for effectively developing contacts that we will talk about in the next chapter. Staying alert to the job market between interviews often finds jobs where you thought there were none. It is an interim activity that rewards those who work at it.

Everything comes to him who
hustles while he waits.
-Thomas Edison

Networking

*Keep away from people who try to
belittle your ambitions. Small people
always do that, but the really great
make you feel that you, too, can
become great. If you want to be
successful, walk and talk with
successful people.*
-Mark Twain

The Value of Networking

You are sending out introduction letters with accompanying
resumés. However, you are unsure whether you have covered
all the opportunities. Maybe you did not notice an emerging company. Maybe another division within the target leading edge
company needs someone. Do you wait to read about it in the next
industry publication? There is a better way to find out what might
be happening. Most people refer to it as *networking*. Unfortunately,
networking has some bad connotations brought on by selfish, rude
people using other people to further their own careers without

reciprocating. That is not networking, that is just being a jerk. Networking is developing and maintaining a connected circle of people who can inform you about job leads or other pertinent industry information. When you are working, networking is important to keep you current on changing trends. However, it is an absolute necessity when you are job hunting. So, it is the next step in the strategy.

Step Seven: Network with People Who Can Inform You

Network with people who can continually inform you about career opportunities. The job market divides into two broad categories: the unpublished market and the published one. The unpublished market holds nearly all of the high-profile jobs. You want to tap this market. The leading edge companies only occasionally advertise their high-value jobs in the newspaper. Why is this the case? These jobs are so important, employers want really good people to fill them. They want people who have been personally recommended by people whose judgment the employer knows firsthand to be good. The employer readily accepts these anointed applicants. The job becomes theirs to lose. Employment agencies and newspaper ads just cannot give the personal guarantee.

Tapping the unpublished market takes work and patience. However, finding the opportunity is only part of the solution. You need to have an insider give you the nod. This means you have to network.

**You Won't Find Many High-Value
Jobs in the Want Ads**

Networking Right

If you go at this hard and aggressively, you will just make people mad, the opposite of what you want to happen. Networking is a directed and persistent building process. The strength of the network is a function of your professionalism, courtesy, and your willingness to reciprocate. Many of the leads and contacts come back on themselves. This is the beauty to the effort.

I started networking so I could find a better job. Well, I got a new job but I still keep up my contacts. Most of them are great people. A few have become good friends. They are almost like my safety net. If I need information or a business favor, I've got people to turn to.
            -Account executive with a computer company

Getting Started

Start by talking about your job search to friends and professors. On the other hand, if you are a practicing attorney, ask other attorneys. Talk to people with whom you feel comfortable. Chances are pretty good these people will not know of any jobs, or much about anything you need to know. However, they will probably know someone who does. These people they know make up the second circle. You are now networking.

I have a friend who paints houses. He knew I was looking for a job after graduation. Well, he was painting the offices of a property management company. The office manager mentioned they needed help in managing one of their properties. Somebody who could deal with people and understood contracts and contractors. My painter friend called me, and I called right before the office manager was going to contact an employment agency. I interviewed, and they hired me at a few thousand more than they were going to pay because they had saved the agency commission. It's a great job with a

lot of potential. You just never know who can help you. I recommend my friend to everybody I meet who needs painting done.
-Property management associate for a national
property management company

The second circle of contacts, and those beyond, are the most useful in your job hunt. But, it's harder to connect as the web expands. You do not know these people. This is where the real work begins—calling these referrals whom you do not personally know. However, you can ease this difficulty with either of these methods:

• Have your referring contact call the referral first, and then you call; or

• Arrange with your referring contact for all three of you to meet.

However, in most cases, you will be calling cold. Do not avoid calling because it may be awkward. Those who keep networking get jobs. So make the call. Call and set up a face-to-face meeting with the referral. Why not just talk to the referral on the phone? Because a person is more likely to help someone they have met. People do not respond the same to just a voice on the phone.

Know what you are going to say before you call. Introduce yourself, briefly explain that you would like some information, and arrange a meeting. Always mention your mutual acquaintance as soon as possible to legitimize your call and your request for time. Do not waste the referral's time. However, if they open up and want to talk further on the phone, that is great. That means that meeting them will be much more relaxed. If not, wait until you meet him or her to say more. Never ask about possible job openings—even if your referring contact knows there is one. Putting people on the spot rarely works to your advantage.

I not only use all the brains I have, but all I can borrow.
-Woodrow Wilson
(unsuccessful solo practitioner and
28th president of the United States)

Meeting the Referral

Before meeting with referrals, call your referring contact back. Thank him or her and explain that you are about to meet their friend. Ask for a little background information on the person. This will make it easier to develop a rapport quickly. Do not underestimate the importance of your initial meeting with your referral. If you know about something important the referral has accomplished, acknowledge it. Honest compliments never hurt. Empty flattery, though, always does. Remember, no matter how well your meeting is going, thirty minutes is enough time to use.

Summarize your objective by explaining the kind of job you want. Inform the referral about your legal training and how it applies. Be positive here. You need to convince the referral because it is this person who may be recommending you for the job to a friend who has an opening. Again, get to the point. You should think about what you are going to say before you go to meet the referral. There should not be any awkward silence. Be an active participant. Personalize your questions when you can. Make the referral feel as if he or she is an integral part of your search. Do not be afraid to ask for specific advice. Most people like to help and everybody likes to give advice. Remember, not only are you looking for potential high-profile career openings, but you are also looking for more people to contact. The referral, too, may not know of a job, but he or she may be able to direct you to someone who does.

> *No one is wise enough by himself.*
> -Titus Maccius Plautus
> (Roman playwright)

Keep Your Network on a Disk—Not in Your Head

Right after every meeting, enter short notes about it into your computer. You should have a file set up to record your meetings, correspondence, and so forth. Organization will help you not miss opportunities. How you set up the file is up to you. Any number of ways will work. Just make sure you know how to get hold of these people when the need arises. When you do talk with them you will know what you previously discussed. Canned software programs are available to help you here if you need them.

Say Thank You

After you have logged in the meeting, always take time to send a thank you note. This is both professional and courteous. They will remember it. Thank the contact for something specific he or she did or told you. No generic thank you notes: personalize them.

Business related thank you notes are a sign of class. I appreciate every one of them I received. And I remember every person that sent one.
-Vice president of an international energy firm

Keep Working on the Network

Once you start getting referrals, you must follow up with them. Keep them active. To follow up, you must continually remind people of you and your job hunt. Maintaining a relationship is far more important to you than it is to them. So do not count on them to stay in touch with you. You strengthen the ties that you have established. Every so often call them or drop them a note to keep them posted. Two of the best ways to follow up are:

• calling with a specific question relating to something you discussed previously or calling to explain how their advice is working out.
• informing them of something that might be of use to them. Suddenly, you are now their contact!

I spend one day a month reconnecting. Some people I call. I drop newspaper articles or magazine articles in the mail that might interest them to others. I always read with an eye for these types of articles. I've helped two of my contact friends get jobs after they lost theirs. That made me feel really good. It's great when they are no longer just contacts—but friends.

-Sales manager for a telecommunications company

Networking into Other Networks

Large, well-formed webs exist for you to tie into. Alumni groups, professional organizations, and trade organizations are examples of prespun webs. Professional organizations are particularly useful because their members are exactly the type of people you want to meet. Trade organizations are a source of industry gossip to find out what companies are doing and who is leading the charge. Use them. Find out if the association has a local office. If not, the following is a partial listing of some of the high-profile career professional organizations. Write to them for information about meetings, membership directories, and so forth.

Attending a professional organization's meetings is a great place to expand your web. However, please be aware that association members often complain about the number of pushy job seekers attending regular meetings. Be careful approaching people. Ask for information, not a job.

Project Finance/Business Development

Financial Executives Institute
P.O. Box 1938
Morristown, NJ 07962-1938

Public Relations

Public Relations Society of America, Inc.
33 Irving Place
New York, NY 10003

Human Resources

International Personnel Management Association
1617 Duke Street
Alexandria, VA 22314

Corporate Trainers

American Society for Training and Development
600 Maryland Avenue, SW
Suite 305
Washington, DC 20025

Publication Editors

American Society of Magazine
  Editors
575 Lexington Avenue
New York, NY 10022

Association of American
  Publishers
220 East 23rd Street
New York, NY 10010

Investment Product Sales Professionals

American Financial Services
  Association
919 18th Street, NW
Washington, DC 20006

National Association of
  Securities Dealers
33 Whitehall Street
New York, NY 10004

Marketing

American Marketing Association
250 South Wacker Drive
Suite 200
Chicago, IL 60606-5819

General Manager/District or Area

American Management Association
135 West 50th Street
New York, NY 10020

Property Management

Institute of Real Estate Management
430 North Michigan Avenue
Chicago, IL 60611

Management Consultants

Institute of Management Consultants
19 West 44th Street
New York, NY 10036

Education Consultants

American Federation of
Teachers
555 New Jersey Avenue, West
Washington, DC 20001

National Education
Association
1201 16th Street, NW
Washington, DC 20036

Networking never ends. The network just expands and gets stronger. Even after you have landed a job and are well into your career, you still will have many of your original contacts, plus many more new ones. Networking takes time and work. Many people do not like to do it, but it is an integral part of the strategy. For a further discussion on networking, refer to Section E of the Appendix for suggested further readings.

All of your efforts to this point are leading to the make-or-break event—the interview. You do well here and you have succeeded. You do poorly, and you have wasted a lot of valuable effort. Let us look at this most important step.

It is no use saying 'we are doing our best.'
You have got to succeed in doing what is necessary.
-Winston Churchill

Chapter Nine

Closing the Sale at the Interview

Think before you speak; pronounce not imperfectly,
nor bring out your words too hastily; but
orderly and distinctly.
-George Washington

Step Eight: Prepare for Every Interview

Prepare for every interview. Close the sale here. Every step in the strategy is taken in order to sit for an interview.

- researching high-profile fields and careers;
- identifying leading edge companies;
- writing introduction letters and resumés; and
- developing a networking of contacts

The interview lands you the job. It is the deciding event in the job search process.

Approach Each Interview with These Points in Mind:

- The interviewer usually decides about you in the first five minutes of the interview. He or she spends the rest of the interview justifying that first impression.
- Your negatives influence the interviewer more than your positives.
- Interviewers assess your interpersonal skills by how you act at the interview.

Interviewing should be a required course in every college. Some graduates have an idea of what to do, but most of them are ill-prepared. Most recruiters I know find the process very tiring. Few applicants prepare for an interview. Most are not really sure what it is they can do or what they want to do. It's no wonder college grads have such a tough time landing a first job.

-Recruiter for a Fortune 500 company

The interview is where you sell yourself, in person, to the company. It is not where you rehash your introduction letter and resumé. Nor is it merely a time to answer questions that an interviewer throws at you. It is for presenting the facts in an organized, confident manner so that you can sell yourself into a job. Which facts do you stress? Focus on the first and second bullets. Your negatives speak louder than your positives and you will not have much time to mute them. Success or failure is a function of how you address these negatives. Initially, the interviewer will view your legal training negatively: you are just waiting to practice law somewhere and will leave at the first opportunity to do so. The letter of introduction should have helped in this regard. However, you will have to convince the interviewer in person. You must be ready to do that. Preparation and practice are essential to success in this task.

Prepare and Practice

You want to come across as confident, knowledgeable, and professional. Do not count on charm to carry the day. Most people will tell you they are not at their best during interviews. By preparing for an interview, you will be calmer, more organized, and sound better during your actual presentation.

With so much at stake, anxiety causes people to perform poorly.

Recheck your web to learn anything new about the company and, if possible, anything about the person who will be interviewing you. Look for information you can use to make yourself sound more knowledgeable, more interested, and better than the other applicants. Think of the ways your background and experience fits with what you have read. Be prepared to show the interviewer how you can contribute. Review your information several times for a few minutes each day before the interview. The more frequently you review, the more you will remember. It takes lots of practicing before you can effectively handle your perceived liabilities and showcase your strengths.

The Interview

Remember, the first five minutes determine your fate. Know what you are going to say before you sit down to the interview. Take what you have learned from your research and form your responses accordingly. Practice responding to the interviewer's anticipated questions and concerns so that your responses become second nature. Interviewers typically focus on, in this order:

- your liabilities;
- your interpersonal skills; and
- your strengths.

Let us attack the most important area—your liabilities.

Handling Liabilities

A liability is any attribute or experience hindering your chance of being offered a job. Now *you* may consider the attribute or experience a strength, but the *interviewer* sees it differently. Never ignore or shrug off a perceived liability. Likewise, never apologize for a perceived liability. Excuses, sob stories, and apologies for liabilities will never improve you chances in an interview. Zero in on the interviewer's concerns and deal with them. You will effectively deal with them because anticipating the questions and practicing the responses has reduced your anxiety and improved the demeanor of your presentation.

Interviewers usually attack your liabilities with direct and pointed questions. They ask these questions to validate their negative opinion. They will ask some or all of these questions:

- Why did you go to law school?
- Why aren't you practicing law?
- Do you want to practice law in the future?
- Why do not you want to practice law any more? Will you go back someday?

> *It is common sense to take a method and try it.*
> *If it fails, admit it frankly and try another,*
> *but above all, try something.*
> -Franklin Roosevelt
> (ex-Wall Street lawyer and 32nd president of the United States)

The interviewer is gauging your interest level and vocational maturity. You must show that you have a high level of both. Focus initially on neutralizing the interviewer's concern. Then quickly go on to show your perceived liability actually will bring value to the employer.

Recent Law Students

First, neutralize the employers concern that you are just biding time until you can land a lawyer job by explaining that you attended law school to prepare for a business career. Mention that well over a quarter of those legally trained never practice law and you intend to add to that statistic. Discuss the financial reasons, the adversarial nature of practicing law, and so forth. Cite that you chose the business sector for the wider range of opportunities for career advancement and financial rewards. Explain your interest in the field and career *with specificity*. Then, show how your legal training will help you perform this *particular* job. You have done this already with the introduction letter.

Most people who didn't attend law school are somewhat intrigued by it. They have an idea of what you learn, but they are really not sure. It's really up to you to educate them about your education. They just do not have a good enough idea to do it for themselves. Most of them are impressed once they realize the broad range of expertise related to business you have. But, again, you have to explain that you do because they do not know. Put your background into terms they understand.

-Manager for an import-export company

Showcasing Strengths

Chapter Two had set forth the attributes of legal training:
- good communication skills
- self-directed
- leadership, as well as team playing capability
- knowledge of and ability to apply the law to the business situation
- constructive thinking skills
- persuasive ability

Mention one or more of these attributes to the interviewer. However, merely mentioning that you have this positive attribute is not going to convince the interviewer that you will be a better performer. You have done that, in part, in the introduction letter. The interviewer needs more. He or she needs to be convinced by you, right then, in person. Show how this attribute contributes to an enhanced performance by showing how it applies to an actual or hypothetical situation that commonly occurs in the job. You must be well versed in the job to be convincing. This story or episode should only take a minute or two to present and should be practiced prior to the interview so that you can present it concisely and in a flowing manner. Do not expect the interviewer to make this connection. They do not have the background to do it. But, even if they did, they are not inclined to make the effort. It is up to you to sell yourself.

The interview that I went on for this job was the first time I tried to illustrate how law school applies to the business world. The interviewer, who is now my boss, was concerned that I wouldn't be a team player. He felt lawyers were kind of egotistical lone wolves.

I really did not know what to say. Then, I started to tell him about how my mock trial partner and I got all the way to the semi-finals. We were not the best students, either one of us. But we worked as a team. We knew what each other's weaknesses were. And we covered for each other. It was like we were one person. That's why we did so well. We surprised the whole class. But we surprised ourselves the most.

I told him I learned the value of teamwork because there will always be smarter people. But, if you work as a team, you can win. The whole can be greater than the sum of the parts.

-Member of a business development team
for an international energy company

I know of no more encouraging fact than the unquestionable ability of man to elevate his life by a conscious endeavor.
-Henry David Thoreau

Changing Careers

The situation will be similar if you are a practicing attorney looking to change careers. The interviewer will be wary of you in two ways:

- that your desire is only temporary; and/or
- you do not have adequate business skills.

Discuss, *generally,* why you are leaving. Next, discuss *specifically* what interests you about this career and company. Cite an actual or hypothetical situation that illustrates how your background skills will benefit the employer in a business situation encountered in *this job.* You may want to expand on what you wrote in the introduction letter. Again, you have to know about the job to make this work. This is why it is important to research the company and the business sector. Annual reports, trade magazines, and Standard & Poor's research material are just some of the information that you should have studied. They provide useful material to dialogue over and show the interviewer that you are a knowledgeable business person.

Many business people do not like lawyers. They think they keep the deal from getting done. All that lawyers do is obstruct. I had an interview with a VP who had just had one of her deals derailed by her legal department over some indemnification language.

So you can imagine what my chances were being a corporate attorney looking to get into the business side. I figured I didn't have much to lose, so I told her that I was never like that. I always wanted to get the deal done as long as it made legal sense. A few months ago, I went with the business development manager and a counterpart from the other side to a sushi bar to see if the deal we were all working on could be salvaged. There really wasn't much hope of that happening. Well, my guy got sick about halfway through the meal. Actually, I wasn't feeling so well either. Anyway, he excused himself and left. I was determined to get this deal because it might kill me anyway. Well, we talked, and as we talked, things began to click. We figured out how both of us could make the deal work. That's how

I became interested in the development side. And, I think I'm pretty good at it. But I still don't like raw fish.

-Business development manager for
a telecommunications firm

Do Not Just Talk About It

What about convincing the interviewer of your interpersonal skills? The interviewer is continuously assessing you as the two of you interact. Telling him or her that you have great communications skills and like dealing with people is unconvincing if you speak tentatively and are ill at ease. It is the old talking-to-your-shoes problem.

I don't understand how applicants can come in and interview for advertising and marketing jobs the way they do. They tell you how great they are at developing rapport, but they're mumbling and staring at their shoes while they tell you! They may be great people and really can do what they say. But, they sure didn't do it when they had an opportunity. Nervousness is not a good excuse. There will be plenty of situations on this job when you will be nervous. That's when I need my people to be poised and outgoing. That's how I make money. And, that's how they make money.

-President of an advertising agency

Most interviewers report that candidates do not sell themselves strongly enough. Instead of taking charge and selling themselves, they only answer questions. They do not really dialogue.

How to Say What You Know to Say

You have prepared and practiced and now it is the time for the actual meeting. Your demeanor is all that is left to work on. The underlying precept is to act professional and confident. Bring your notes to review while waiting. Do not just sit there and stare into space. Always bring extra copies of your introduction letter and resumé. This shows the interviewer you plan for contingencies.

Start the interview with a warm but professional tone and maintain it throughout. Speak firmly and confidently. Maintain an upright posture. Do not slump in your chair. You must exude confidence, poise, and assertiveness during those critical first few minutes. This does not mean trying to control the interview. It just means actively participating in it. Build rapport and connect with the interviewer. Let him or her set the stage so you can get a sense of where they are coming from. Follow their lead and do not jump ahead. Pay attention and you will discover that certain nuances, thoughts, and opinions more strongly impress than others. When the interview is over, it is those subtle connections, as much as the right answers, that the interviewers remember. With preparation and practice in hand, you should be beaming with confidence.

Questions Are Just as Important as Answers

The interviewer expects you to ask some questions. Not doing so usually leads to a rejection. It implies you require very little information to make a career decision, and maybe, very little to make a business decision. Utilize the research you have done to formulate three or four questions specific to the company. The following areas are appropriate to discuss:

- How do you see my position developing in response to competition from _____?
- Can you tell me about my prospective coworkers?
- How would you like to see my position develop in light of the new products or services being developed by the company?

It's always disheartening to get all the way through the interview and think this applicant is great. You ask them if they have any questions. They just shake their head. It's as if you've bored them and they want to get out of there. That always sticks with me.

-Human resources manager

Again, you are striving for dialogue, not a question and answer session. Do not ask anything about salary or benefits. Once you get an offer, you can talk about those things. Most interviewers are not up on the benefits package anyway. Show interest in the company's success through your questions. Remember, you are still selling, even now.

> *We must cultivate our garden.*
> -Voltaire
> (eighteenth-century French poet and historian)

Close the interview by reiterating how interested you are in the job and how you appreciated the opportunity to talk about your qualifications. Let the interviewer know that you are willing to talk further at a later date. Do not let your energy level drop here. Leave a positive impression.

Getting Ready for the Next One

What if the interview went poorly? Well, if nothing else, a bad interview prepares you for the next one. You do not become an expert interviewer after just one interview. It takes a while before you become comfortable with the process. Learn from your mistakes and do better the next time. There will always be more opportunities. The dynamic business sector makes certain of that.

> *Experience is not what happens to a man; it is*
> *what a man does with what happens to him.*
> -Aldous Huxley
> (early-twentieth-century English novelist)

The Thank You Note

The reasons for writing a thank you note are that most interviewers expect it. Three brief paragraphs will do. The first thanks the interviewer for seeing you. Do not overdo it. Next, succinctly recap how you specifically can help the company. Lastly, inform the interviewer you will be calling on the phone. Give a date on which you will call. Do not let more than one day pass without writing the note.

Your Reward

You have had a great interview. The job seems perfect for you and you perfect for it. A few days later, the interviewer calls you and offers you the high-profile job. Congratulations! You have done it! You have shown there is no substitute for a well thought out plan and hard work in getting a job. This is certainly true once you are on the job.

The Final Step: Follow Through

Once you are in your new career, follow through on what you said. Hopefully, this will be your ending. You have a great background and a big world in front of you. Take advantage of it. Before we part, I would like to visit a little bit more with the practicing attorney who is contemplating changing careers.

The good days are today, and better
days are coming tomorrow. Our greatest
songs are still unsung.
-Hubert Humphrey

Epilogue

All this will not be finished in the first one hundred days. Nor will it be finished in the first thousand days, nor in the life of this Administration, nor even perhaps in our lifetime on this planet. But let us begin.
-John F. Kennedy

In Closing

Whether you read this book straight through and take action upon completion or you work step-by-step, the important element is action. You must act upon this knowledge in order to give it value. I reiterate the strategy and the steps implementing it below. Now, it is up to you.

The Strategy

Define the career you want in terms of your legal training. Show your legal training has given you valuable business sector skills.

Implementing the Strategy

1. Assure yourself that a successful business career can be superior to practicing law.
2. You possess the traits of a high-value worker. Showcase your legal training.
3. Identify high-value careers within high-value fields and relate your skills and interests to them.
4. Target the triple points: a high-value career in a high-value field with a leading edge company.
5. Contact your triple point target with an introduction letter accompanied by a resumé.
6. Define your career selection in terms of your legal training and experience.
7. Develop a network with people who can continually inform you about the career opportunities.
8. Prepare for every interview. Close the sale here.
9. Once you are in your new career, follow through on what you said.

It is up to you to adapt the information presented in this book to your own personal situation. I realize the solution I have presented is not quick and easy. It requires quite a bit of work. However, intuitively you know there really are not any shortcuts when it comes to important areas of your life. Your career is an important facet of your life. In part, it will describe you. You are responsible for your career. No one has as much interest in the outcome of it as you. No one has as much control over it as you. Make it the career you want.

If we did all the things we are capable of
doing we would literally astound ourselves.
-Thomas Edison

Appendix

Section A: Questions to Help the Law Student Determine a Preferred Career Situation

The following questions should give you a good idea of the career environment where you would be most comfortable. Answer the questions and wait a few days and answer the second set of identical questions without looking at your first set of answers. If your answers match, you are ready to move on. If they do not, reconcile your answers before moving on.

Set No. 1

1. Do I enjoy working on projects or ventures that may take months to bring to resolution? Or, am I more happy working where the transaction times are much shorter, like daily or weekly?

2. Am I comfortable with spending a lot of my time working with financial models for projects or businesses? Am I comfortable using the computer?

3. Do I prefer working more with numbers than people? Or, do I enjoy making the effort to meet new people?

4. Do I prefer working with concepts rather that details? Or, am I a detail-oriented person?

5. Do I enjoy traveling? How much of the month would I tolerate being out of town? Or, out of the country?

6. In what area is my undergraduate training? Do I enjoy that field? Why or why not?

7. In what area of business do I have experience? Did I enjoy that experience? Why or why not?

Set No. 2

1. Do I enjoy working on projects or ventures that may take months to bring to resolution? Or, am I more happy working where the transaction times are much shorter, like daily or weekly?

2. Am I comfortable with spending a lot of my time working with financial models for projects or businesses? Am I comfortable using the computer?

3. Do I prefer working more with numbers than people? Or, do I enjoy making the effort to meet new people?

4. Do I prefer working with concepts rather that details? Or, am I a detail-oriented person?

5. Do I enjoy traveling? How much of the month would I tolerate being out of town? Or, out of the country?

6. In what area is my undergraduate training? Do I enjoy that field? Why or why not?

7. In what area of business do I have experience? Did I enjoy that experience? Why or why not?

Section B: Questions to Help the Practicing Attorney Determine a Preferred Career Situation

The instructions are the same as for the law student. The following questions should give you a good idea of the career environment where you would be most comfortable. Answer the questions and wait a few days and answer the second set of identical questions without looking at your first set of answers. If your answers match, you are ready to move on. If they do not, reconcile your answers before moving on.

Set No. 1

1. Do I enjoy working on projects or ventures that may take months to bring to resolution? Or, am I more happy working where the transaction times are much shorter, like daily or weekly?

2. How are my computer skills? Am I comfortable working with spreadsheets? With presentation software? Am I willing to upgrade my computer skills?

3. Do I enjoy making the effort to meet new people? With what types of people am I comfortable?

4. Do I prefer working with concepts rather than details? Or, am I a detail-oriented person?

5. If I do very little traveling now, am I willing to start traveling? What about international travel?

6. If I am a very highly paid attorney, am I willing to accept a reduction in my income for a period of time? How much and for how long?

7. In what area of business do I have experience? In what area are my contacts with the business sector?

Set No. 2

1. Do I enjoy working on projects or ventures that may take months to bring to resolution? Or, am I more happy working where the transaction times are much shorter, like daily or weekly?

2. How are my computer skills? Am I comfortable working with spreadsheets? With presentation software? Am I willing to upgrade my computer skills?

3. Do I enjoy making the effort to meet new people? With what types of people am I comfortable?

4. Do I prefer working with concepts rather than details? Or, am I a detail-oriented person?

5. If I do very little traveling now, am I willing to start traveling? What about international travel?

6. If I am a very highly paid attorney, am I willing to accept a reduction in my income for a period of time? How much and for how long?

7. In what area of business do I have experience? In what area are my contacts with the business sector?

Section C: Identifying Leading Edge Companies

Use the following questions to determine leading edge companies in the specified high-value field.

Field: _____

- Which companies seem to lead the pack in innovation?

- Which companies are always in the news?

- Which companies have strong earnings?

- Which companies are expanding? Is the expansion into new geographic markets or into new product lines?

- How do the companies seem to differentiate themselves from the others in the field?

Field: _____

- Which companies seem to lead the pack in innovation?

- Which companies are always in the news?

- Which companies have strong earnings?

- Which companies are expanding? Is the expansion into new geographic markets or into new product lines?

- How do the companies seem to differentiate themselves from the others in the field?

Field: _____

- Which companies seem to lead the pack in innovation?

- Which companies are always in the news?

- Which companies have strong earnings?

- Which companies are expanding? Is the expansion into new geographic markets or into new product lines?

- How do the companies seem to differentiate themselves from the others in the field?

Section D: Introduction Letter and Resumé Writing Worksheets

These worksheet pages are provided as a guide for collecting and distilling relevant, information for each of your target companies. You may make multiple copies of these pages so that you will have one set for each of your targets.

Worksheet A compiles general information about you such as employment history and education. Worksheet B compiles information about the target company and information about you that relates to what you have learned about the target company's activities and special needs. Research creatively. You need to identify a need and then show the target employer how *you* will fill that need.

Worksheet A

General Personal Information
Employment History

Dates: _____

Job Title: _____

Employer Name: _____

Address: _____

Dates: _____

Job Title: _____

Employer Name: _____

Address: _____

Dates: _____

Job Title: _____

Employer Name: _____

Address: _____

Education

Undergraduate: _____

_____

Law School: _____

Worksheet B

Target Company Name:

_____

Address:

_____

_____

Contact Person:

_____

Target Job:

_____

Date Resumé Mailed:

_____

Follow-up Contact Date:

_____

General Information and Noteworthy Activities of the Company

_____

_____

_____

_____

_____

_____

_____

_____

_____

_____

_____

_____

Job Skills Required

_____

_____

_____

_____

_____

_____

_____

_____

_____

_____

_____

_____

_____

Employer Need(s)

_____
_____
_____
_____
_____
_____
_____
_____

My Relevant Accomplishments

_____
_____
_____
_____
_____
_____
_____
_____

My Relevant Skills and How They Were Attained

_____
_____
_____
_____
_____
_____
_____
_____

How I Will Fill the Need and Add Value

_____

_____

_____

_____

_____

_____

_____

_____

_____

Section E: Suggested Further Reading

These books provide further explanation of the topics covered in this book. They may provide you with ideas as you develop and implement the strategy to help you select an exciting and rewarding career path.

Chapter One: You Are Not Alone

The following books discuss the changing dynamics of the American economy.

Chapman, Robert, Miriam Johnson, and Richard Wegmann, *Work in the New Economy: Career and Job Seeking Into the 21st Century.* American Association for Counseling and Development, 1989.

Handy, Charles, *The Age of Paradox.* Harvard Business School Press, Boston, Massachusetts, 1994.

United States Department of Labor, *Occupational Outlook Handbook 1996–97 Edition.* VGM Career Horizons, Lincolnwood, Illinois, 1996.

Chapter Two: Can I Do Anything Else Except Practice Law?

The following books discuss the adaptability and value of legal training to other career paths.

Arron, Deborah, *Running From the Law: Why Good Lawyers Are Getting Out of the Legal Profession.* Ten Speed Press, Berkeley California, 1991.

Cain, George, *Turning Points: New Paths and Second Careers for Lawyers.* American Bar Association, Chicago, Illinois, 1994.

Henslee, William D. and Gary A. Munneke, *Nonlegal Careers for Lawyers, Third Edition.* American Bar Association Law Student Division, Chicago, Illinois, 1994.

Sinetar, Marsha, *Do What You Love, The Money Will Follow.* Dell Publishing Company, New York, New York, 1987.

Tieger, Paul D., and Barbara Barron-Tieger, *Do What You Are, Second Edition.* Little, Brown and Company, New York, New York, 1995.

Chapter Three: Second Year and Second Thoughts?

The following books discuss law school life and the opportunities available to law school graduates.

Arron, Deborah, *Running From the Law: Why Good Lawyers Are Getting Out of the Legal Profession.* Ten Speed Press, Berkeley California, 1991.

Munneke, Gary, *Barron's Guide to Law Schools.* Barron's Educational Series, Inc., Hauppauge, New York, 1994.

Sinetar, Marsha, *Do What You Love, The Money Will Follow.* Dell Publishing Company, New York, New York, 1987.

Tieger, Paul D., and Barbara Barron-Tieger, *Do What You Are, Second Edition.* Little, Brown and Company, New York, New York, 1995.

Chapter Four: The Perils of Practice

The following books discuss the career problems encountered by some practicing attorneys and the alternate career paths available to them.

Arron, Deborah, *Running From the Law: Why Good Lawyers Are Getting Out of the Legal Profession.* Ten Speed Press, Berkeley California, 1991.

Bell, Susan, *Full Disclosure: Do You Really Want to Be a Lawyer?* Peterson's Guides, Princeton, New Jersey, 1992.

Cain, George, *Turning Points: New Paths and Second Careers for Lawyers.* American Bar Association, Chicago, Illinois, 1994.

Henslee, William D. and Gary A. Munneke, *Nonlegal Careers for Lawyers, Third Edition.* American Bar Association Law Student Division, Chicago, Illinois, 1994.

Lewis, Adele and David A. Saltman, *Better Resumes for Attorneys and Paralegals.* Barron's Educational Series, Inc., Hauppauge, New York, 1986.

Chapter Five: Research and Redevelopment

These books discuss high-value careers for the coming millennium.

Dent, Harry S. Jr., *The Great Jobs Ahead.* Hyperion Publishing, New York, New York, 1995.
Farr, J. Michael, *America's Fastest Growing Jobs, Third Edition.* Jist Works, Inc., Indianapolis, Indiana, 1995.
Fischgrund, Tom, ed., *The INSIDERS's Guide to the Top 20 Careers in Business & Management.* McGraw Hill, New York, New York, 1994.
Harkavy, Michael, *101 Careers: A Guide to the Fastest-Growing Opportunities.* John Wiley & Sons, Inc., New York, New York, 1990.
United States Department of Labor, *Occupational Outlook Handbook 1996–97 Edition.* VGM Career Horizons, Lincolnwood, Illinois, 1996.

Chapter Six: Seeking the Triple Point

These books discuss high-value business sectors and leading edge companies.

Krannich, Caryl Rae and Ronald L. Krannich, *The Best Jobs for the 1990's and Into the 21st Century.* Impact Publications, Manassas Park, Virginia, 1993.
Lucht, John, *Rites of Passage at $100,000+: Guide to Executive Job-Changing.* The Viceroy Press, New York, New York, 1995.
Peterson's Hidden Job Market 1996 5th Edition. Selected from Corporate Technology Information Services Database, Princetown, New Jersey, 1996.

United States Department of Labor. *Occupational Outlook Handbook 1996–97 Edition.* VGM Career Horizons, Lincolnwood, Illinois, 1996.

Chapter Seven: Making Contact

These books discuss the dynamics of writing introduction letters and resumés.

Beatty, Richard, *175 High Impact Cover Letters 2nd Edition.* John Wiley & Sons, New York, New York, 1996.

Krannich, Caryl Rae and Ronald L. Krannich. *Dynamite Cover Letters & Other Great Job Search Letters!* Impact Publications, Manassas Park, Virginia, 1994.

Lewis, Adele and David A. Saltman, *Better Resumes for Attorneys and Paralegals.* Barron's Educational Series, Inc., Hauppauge, New York, 1986.

Lucht, John, *Rites of Passage at $100,000+: Guide to Executive Job-Changing.* The Viceroy Press, New York, New York, 1995.

Montag, William. *Best Resumes & Cover Letters: Best Resumes for $75,000+ Executive Jobs.* John Wiley & Sons, New York, New York, 1992.

Petras, Kathryn and Ross Petras. *The Only Job Hunting Guide You'll Ever Need: The Most Comprehensive Guide for Job Hunters and Career Switchers, Updated and Revised.* Simon and Schuster, New York, New York, 1995.

Weinstein, Bob. *Resumes Don't Get Jobs: The Realities and Myths of Job Hunting.* McGraw Hill, Inc., New York, New York, 1993.

Chapter Eight: Networking

These books discuss the importance of and techniques useful for networking.

Beatty, Richard, *Job Search Networking.* Bob Adams, Inc., Holbrook, Massachusetts, 1994.

Lucht, John, *Rites of Passage at $100,000+: Guide to Executive Job-Changing*. The Viceroy Press, New York, New York, 1995.

Petras, Kathryn and Ross Petras, *The Only Job Hunting Guide You'll Ever Need: The Most Comprehensive Guide for Job Hunters and Career Switchers, Updated and Revised*. Simon and Schuster, New York, New York, 1995.

Richardson, Douglas, *Networking*. The Wall Street Journal, National Business Employment Weekly. John Wiley & Sons, Inc., New York, New York, 1994.

Chapter Nine: Closing the Sale at the Interview

These books discuss the art of interviewing and provide many useful techniques.

Kanter, Arnold B., *The Essential Book of Interviewing: Everything to Know from Both Sides of the Table*. Times Books, New York, New York, 1995.

Petras, Kathryn and Ross Petras, *The Only Job Hunting Guide You'll Ever Need: The Most Comprehensive Guide for Job Hunters and Career Switchers, Updated and Revised*. Simon and Schuster, New York, New York, 1995.